Best wishes
to Catherine

Meeting Special Education
A Scottish Perspecti

Series Editors

Gwynedd Lloyd and Judith Watson

Volume Five

Working with Communication Difficulties

Edited by Judith Watson

Moray House Publications
1994

Published by Moray House Institute of Education,
Holyrood Road, Edinburgh EH8 8AQ

First published 1994
ISBN 0 901 58063 5

Printed and bound in Great Britain by
BPC – AUP Aberdeen Ltd.

Contents

Introduction

Judith Watson

THE SERIES OF collections of papers entitled **Meeting Special Educational Needs: A Scottish Perspective** was officially launched by the appearance of Volume One in January 1992. Gwynedd Lloyd and I as co-editors believed that there was a need for the publication of some of the exciting educational practice and thinking currently taking place in Scotland. We noted that features of the educational scene in Scotland are frequently neglected in British publications although they have important implications, and that much of the work concerning special educational needs by researchers and practitioners is not publicised or known even in Scotland. The positive responses from a broad range of readers and reviewers have supported the initiative but possibly most gratifying have been changes in thinking and practice that have been reported to us.

The present collection of papers concerns the area of special educational need associated with difficulties in communication, and focuses on pupils whose general ability is within the usual range. There are several reasons why the time seems right for such a theme.

First, there has been a growth in special educational provision in this area reflecting of course changes in policy and awareness at influential levels. During the early 1980s there was a rapid increase in the setting up of specialised 'language units' from the handful that existed in Scotland before this time. More recently there has been the setting up of a special residential school, and the provision or planning in several Scottish Regions for pupils whose communication problems place them somewhere along the continuum of autism. There has also been an increase in groups of parents who have stated their concerns about educational provision for their children very effectively.

Further evidence of the interest in this area of special educational need is the financial support by the Scottish Office Education Department for reports and literature reviews on *Children with Language and Communication Disorders* (Donaldson, 1992) and *Children with Autism* (Aitken et al., 1993), and a research investigation into the role of speech and language therapists with pupils who have special educational needs. In sum, the area has a relatively high profile within educational thinking and in the broader public domain.

At a theoretical level, there is, I believe, more congruence now between findings from research on language acquisition and much of the practice in language intervention. The emphasis in much current research on the development of language in children is on its social interactive nature. The context is recognised as being an important influence on the child's comprehension, and prelinguistic development is seen as continuous with later developing communication skills. Moreover meaningful everyday experiences with responsive adults and peers are shown to be highly motivating and fruitful learning situations, and parents and peers are given due recognition as vitally important communicative partners. Multidisciplinary assessment in a range of contexts is increasingly advocated and practised. These general trends and influences may be seen in many of the contributions to this book.

The thirteen papers that make up Volume Five of the series **Meeting Special Educational Needs: A Scottish Perspective** fall roughly into two groups, with however, many links and common references. The first six papers address issues of identification, assessment and the placement decisions that follow. In the second half of the book papers focus more on practice and pedagogy. Both parts contain illustrative case studies and research findings and contributors include teachers, speech therapists, educational psychologists and academic researchers. The joint authorship of several papers reflects the reality of interprofessional collaboration especially evident in this area of special educational provision.

There is coverage of a wide age range, from toddlers to young adults. All have some form of communication difficulty, but without greatly delayed intellectual development. Pupils with more severe learning difficulties are the focus of another volume in this series. Deafness, such a large area of concern, is not included. Some of the pupils described here have obvious physical impairments, as in chapters 6 and 10; others have less obvious difficulty in motor planning and sequencing, or comprehension problems. Several chapters focus on such pupils within language unit provision, whereas others consider attempts to meet such pupils' special educational needs within mainstream education.

Several authors address the perennially problematic questions of terminology and classification in the area of language and communication difficulties, and Greg McMillan in the opening chapter points out the parallel with the term 'specific learning disability'. Whether medical, linguistic or functional labels are applied in practice will of course depend on a person's training and background. There is general acceptance that there are three basic groupings of difficulty, to do with expression, comprehension and appropriate use, and that many pupils will have difficulty in more than one area. As Greg McMillan points out there is further disagreement concerning the validity of the distinction between language delay and disorder, although this is widely regarded as useful by practitioners.

Anne Macdonald also addresses basic issues invoking the powerful principles of empowerment and enablement for the pupil with communication difficulties. She points out that a balance has to be achieved between the pupils' right to participate in the curriculum and social experience of a mainstream setting, and their need, which cannot be denied, to acquire the communicative competence necessary for such participation. Her discussion of developments in provision in Dundee illustrates one way of attempting to achieve this balance.

Two chapters describe assessment and remediation in what are often seen as rather esoteric areas, both of them fundamental to a child's educational success. Dorothea Bogle considers phonological development and gives guidelines on when there is cause for concern and suggestions for classroom activities. Anne O'Hare elucidates the term dyspraxia, and describes the development of writing. Developmentally a sequence is often observed in the pupil's dominant difficulty, from slow speech at preschool, through reading difficulties at about seven years, and later writing difficulties. The links between early language problems and later ones in reading and writing have often been obscured by the tendency to consider reading and writing skills as specific, and not continuous with early oral communication.

Donaldson and Reid address concerns central to all practitioners. Decisions on appropriate pedagogy and placement must of course depend on beliefs about the likely efficacy of different kinds of intervention. An eclectic approach is embraced and advocated by many practitioners, although their practice can usually be identified as either predominantly behavioural (clearly structured with preset and specified objectives) or more naturalistic (with the emphasis on following the child's lead and interest). The authors point out that judgements about efficacy of placement or teaching approaches are extremely difficult to make with confidence; situations are complex, children all differ and comparisons are often invalid. But the practice of functionally effective communication in everyday activities, generalised at home and with peers at play, must remain a major means to successful confident language use. Whether placement in a language unit is the optimal solution for many children is an open question to which alternatives have also been suggested in the first two chapters.

Alison MacDonald and Caroline Rendle's research beautifully exemplifies assessment and decision making processes in practice, with a group of pupils many might have considered rather young for introduction to microtechnology and augmentative communication. Judged likely not to be able to develop oral communication in the usual way, the two year olds' cognitive, social and physical development formed the basis of an individualised therapy programme using games and microtechnology. Importantly this was always with the participation of a parent. The encouraging results and descriptions of activities form a bridge into the second part of the book.

Chapters by Margaret Mason and by Edward Jefferies and Sally Dolan each describe research central to the use by teachers of the SOED 5-14 guidelines concerning the earliest stages of English Language. Margaret Mason discusses in detail the performance of six pupils with a range of difficulties in communication, in the strands Listening/Watching, Talking, Reading, and Writing. Several problems in the interpretation and use of the attainment targets with her pupils were identified. As she says, it is very important that there should be a way of incorporating the very detailed assessment information which is available on pupils into the framework of the guidelines.

Jefferies and Dolan observed teachers' encouragement of talking in ordinary primary classrooms by examining the contexts and activities in which the four most reticent pupils talked in each of the six classes observed. Among much of interest is the indication that the exploration of teachers' and pupils' views about the value and purpose of classroom talk could form the basis of valuable collaborative staff development. Teachers do not often have opportunities to observe others in action, still less themselves, and this research indicates how rewarding such experiences can be. The joint paper by a teacher and speech therapist describes a pupil with whom they worked together. Mo Townson and Margaret McGregor's collaboration began with assessment and continued with joint planning and evaluation, in a fruitful partnership which is only possible when the two professional groups most directly in contact with pupils understand, value, and communicate well with each other. This paper also raises the important question of following up pupils once they have been reintegrated from units. It is well known that many continue to have learning difficulties.

Collaboration continues to be an important feature of the last four chapters, all of which have wide application to a range of possible settings. Linda Booth and Peter Gregor show how the extreme writing difficulties experienced by pupils with a range of special educational needs were alleviated to a most encouraging extent. The personal word stores and self pacing integral to PAL must contribute in no small measure to pupils' greatly increased motivation and satisfaction. Where previously pupils had opted out they were now reported to be determined and enthusiastic. Keith Topping's work on peer tutoring is well known. Here he describes how oracy can be promoted by activities in which the pupils' communicative partner is not the teacher, but a parent or peer. Positive results have been frequently reported from reading programmes and small group problem solving and discussion activities but there has been less research on oracy. It may be that language units, with their high ratio of adults to pupils, and very small numbers along with the emphasis on adult–pupil dialogue, are less likely to organise tutoring of this kind unless staff are convinced of the effectiveness of this approach. As Keith Topping points out there are potentially great advantages in the use of such methods, especially in the reduction of teacher control (with its widely reported unintentional inhibiting effects) and increased generalisation beyond the classroom.

My own contribution focuses on ways in which teacher talk and planned curricular activities can encourage pupils to be more reflective in the classroom, and how this increased awareness can help their communications.

Along with other authors Keith Topping emphasises fun and enjoyment within the classroom, and this is one of the elements that make up the ethos described by Judith Scott, as conducive to communication. Judith elucidates the currently popular notion of ethos, and the attempts to describe and identify it, and uses examples of classroom dialogue to illustrate its effect on pupils. It is fitting that her concluding chapter describes interactions between teachers and pupils and that there are several echoes back to themes from earlier papers. The most prominent is respect: for pupils, for what they say and think, however haltingly, and for who they are. An ethos which conveys this about pupils will also be one that facilitates their communication.

References

Aitken, K., Papoudi, D., Robarts, J. and Trevarthen, C. (1993) *Children with Autism*. Edinburgh, ECRCD/Edinburgh University

Donaldson, M. L. (1992) *Children with Language and Communication Disorders: A Review of the Literature*. Edinburgh, ECRCD/Edinburgh University

Psychological Assessment and Specific Language Difficulties

Gregor McMillan

This chapter deals with some issues involved in the identification, assessment and education of children with specific language handicaps from the perspective of an educational psychologist. This involves some discussion of theoretical, philosophical and practical aspects of classification, testing and placement. In the main the focus will be on young children with difficulties of sufficient severity to be considered as special educational needs.

Types and categorisation of speech and language difficulty

While children's problems with speech and language are rarely neatly parcelled into discrete areas it is possible to identify three broad areas of difficulty.

1. Expressive language: difficulties in this area include problems with the production of sounds, with the organisation of sounds and grammatical structures and with the acquisition of vocabulary. Some children have difficulty with all of these skills.
2. Receptive language: difficulties in this area are associated with the understanding of language.
3. Semantic/pragmatic skills: some children may have problems with the meaning and use of language in social settings. Autism is sometimes subsumed under the broad category of semantic pragmatic difficulty, but is more frequently treated as a disorder in its own right.

Clearly children who have difficulty with speech and language are children who have not mastered some aspects of skills such as articulation, vocabulary acquisition or the use of language in real life settings. It might seem that the identification of such children would be quite straightforward. However there are difficulties. In the normal preschool population there is a very wide variation in the rate of acquisition of language skills. One child at the age of three might have vocabulary skills which are superior to those of another child of four or even five, without either child being in any sense abnormal. In addition many children who do have delayed speech and language also have other difficulties such as deafness, mental handicap, cerebral palsy, or social or emotional problems. Such children may undoubtedly have language handicaps but they do not have a primary or 'specific' language handicap.

It is common, particularly among speech therapists, to distinguish between language delay and language disorder. This distinction suggests that children with language delay are progressing along normal lines, albeit more slowly than their peers, whereas children with a language disorder have a deviant and atypical acquisition process. It is not, however, clear that such a deviant pattern of acquisition actually exists. Ingram (1987), for example, suggests that with the lack of a clear theory of the extent of individual variation in normal phonological acquisition it is impossible to develop categories of deviant phonology. Ingram suggests that all children fall along a continuum regarding the relation between phonological stage and vocabulary. Children, therefore, who are described as having deviant or disordered phonology, are simply children with a phonological delay but a relatively advanced vocabulary. Berger (1987) points out that the term language disorder is really just a way of indicating that there is something 'not expected' in language behaviours. He also notes that many clinical terms such as 'aphasia' and 'specific language disorder' are essentially summary descriptions and that there may be little justification for the frequent associated presumption that unusual features of language are a result of disorder or pathology in the underlying specific mechanisms that generate language.

In Lothian Region, where I work, there is a clear policy that language units, which are small class groups attached to mainstream primary schools, are intended for pupils with 'specific speech and language difficulties' and that other children, whose language difficulties are deemed secondary to broader impairments are not appropriate for such units. Pupils with specific language difficulties are defined as having severe difficulties with some aspect of speech and language but non-verbal reasoning abilities within the normal range. While this is a common practice in most education authorities, Donaldson (1991) points out that this policy is not necessarily theoretically justifiable or, indeed, adhered to in practice. She points out that the degree to which linguistic development is constrained by intellectual development is unclear and that there is evidence that children with 'global' impairments may benefit from language unit provision. In fact, by accident or design, substantial number of children with general cognitive delays have found themselves in language units. The degree to which this may benefit such children is, no doubt, chiefly related to the suitability of the curriculum offered to them. Bishop and Edmundson (1987) found that children with average non-verbal intellectual abilities did tend to make more rapid progress in language than children with general cognitive delays.

The concept of specific language difficulties

The task of identifying children with specific language handicaps begins to look less straightforward. No longer is one looking to simply establish that a child has a difficulty with language. The task now is to identify a child with a severe language delay (or disorder!) whose difficulties cannot be attributed to physical, intellectual, emotional or sensory impairments and whose non-verbal abilities are within the normal range. For many psychologists and teachers this definition of specific language difficulty may sound eerily familiar. This is, of course, because a simple substitution of the phrase 'specific learning difficulties' for 'specific language difficulties' provides us with the popular definition of 'dyslexia'. Indeed the parallels between dyslexia and specific language difficulties are striking. In both cases a 'condition', usually of no known aetiology, is identified largely by exclusion criteria. In other words, it is defined by ruling out a range of possible causative factors rather than by identifying such factors. Educationally special provision is set up and access is restricted to a residual group after much larger numbers of equally handicapped children have been deemed ineligible. Furthermore and conversely there is a plethora of dubious medical and psychological research (see Young and Tyre, 1983) purporting to find underlying neurological and psycho-physical correlates and causes of the conditions, such as 'sequencing difficulties'. Finally there is the ever present trap of the circular argument, whereby observation becomes condition becomes cause. This inappropriate use of the medical model can lead to assertions such as 'he can't read because he's dyslexic' or 'she can't talk properly because she's got a language handicap'. While not wishing to denigrate the research into the causes of such problems in children, it is important to remember that, at present, terms such as dyslexia and specific language difficulty are chiefly descriptive labels. The children who attend the language unit where I work are children of normal intellectual ability who have difficulties with some aspects of language and communication. Stating that they have a specific language handicap is simply a brief way of saying this.

Crystal (1984) points out that the term 'specific learning (or language) difficulty' is not only simply a label, it is also a misleading label. Crystal accepts that it is reasonable to describe a significant discrepancy between a child's actual level of psycholinguistic functioning and the level which might be expected given normal intelligence and sensory capability as a specific language disability. However he goes on to suggest that there are few concepts more unspecific than specific language disability, which may encompass problems of cognition, speech, motor control and planning, reading and spelling, memory, perception and attention and the web of relations between such factors. Crystal indeed suggests that a more appropriate label might be 'unspecific language disability'.

Semantic-pragmatic difficulties and autism

The situation becomes even more complicated when one considers the group of children with semantic pragmatic difficulties, who are also deemed to have a specific language handicap. Such children may have quite well developed grammar, phonology, articulation and vocabulary, but great difficulty in actually communicating effectively in a social context. As McTear and Conti-Ramsden (1992) point out such children often have difficulty with conversation, making friends and coping with everyday social interactions. Commonly they make odd associations, tangential or inappropriate remarks, may pay undue attention to literal meaning, have problems with descriptions of everyday events that are related temporarily or causally and may have poor social skills.

The picture is further complicated by the view of some workers that autism is a part of a continuum of semantic-pragmatic disorder and that autistic children are simply children with a severe version of this difficulty. However Aarons and Gittens (1992) see autism itself as a continuum. They make the crucial point that the majority of autistic children are also severely mentally handicapped. There is certainly some relationship between the kind of difficulties described above as characteristic of semantic-pragmatic difficulties and Lorna Wing's (1988) 'triad of impairments of social interaction' which characterise autism – impairments of social recognition, social communication and social understanding and imagination. Once again it is important to remember that terms such as 'autism' and 'semantic-pragmatic difficulties' are essentially descriptive labels and debates about whether children have one or the other are essentially sterile. However, language units in Lothian Region admit children of normal intelligence with autistic or semantic-pragmatic difficulties and it is, therefore, necessary to identify such a group. It is perhaps ironic, in view of the importance of the concept of primary, specific language handicap in placement, that McTear and Conti-Ramsden (1992) note that there is some doubt as to whether pragmatic difficulties are a type of primary language handicap or are a reflection of a more general cognitive deficit.

It may seem that the process of identification of specific categories of handicap is contrary to the spirit of the 1981 Education Act and the Warnock Report with their emphasis on assessment of special educational need rather than placement by categorisation. However, Rutter (1978) showed, for example, that IQ scores were as good a predictor of future educational attainment in autistic as in non-autistic children. The educational needs of a severely mentally handicapped autistic child or a severely mentally handicapped child with profound language difficulties may be very different from those of a bright child with phonological or pragmatic difficulties. I will return to some of these issues after discussing assessment procedures.

Diagnostic assessment

The fundamental task of an educational psychologist in initially assessing a child is to decide:

1. does the child have special education needs, i.e. needs which could not be met within a normally resourced mainstream classroom,
2. what are these SENs, and
3. how should they best be met?

Obviously in the case of children with language handicaps, as with other problems, this is a multidisciplinary process, with the views and assessment of speech therapists being of particular importance. Generally a comprehensive assessment of a child with a language handicap (pre-placement) should include a detailed medical assessment, preferably by a paediatrician specialising in this field; a speech therapy assessment and a psychological assessment. If the child attends a school or nursery, teaching staff can provide invaluable information about the child's functioning in familiar real life settings. Obviously all professionals will involve parents in the assessment process and will rely heavily on parents' reports of their child's language skills at home.

Insofar as children with specific language handicap are defined as being intellectually within the normal range, for the purposes of entry to a language unit, it is an important function of the psychologist to assess the intellectual abilities of the child. Donaldson (1991) points out that the aim of identifying children with language disorders is usually best served by using norm referenced tests, including IQ tests. She specifically mentions the WISC(R) (Weschler, 1974) and the British Ability Scales (Elliot, Murray and Pearson, 1978). The use of psychometric testing is deeply unfashionable in educational psychology at present, partly as a reaction to the excessive use of such instruments in the 1960s and 1970s. In my view there is no substitute for formal intellectual testing in the investigation of language handicap. Unfortunately in current professional training courses psychologists are now often given little information on the use of such tests. I think that psychometric tests are essential in, for example, distinguishing between a child with a global mental handicap and a child with a specific language disorder. Criterion referenced assessment is unlikely to be helpful in this area. It is, of course, possible to maintain that an accurate estimate of intellectual ability and cognitive development can be made through structured observation, the use of play materials in naturalistic settings, parental interviews and so on. However, while it may be possible to broadly distinguish between normal and handicapped groups using informal methods, it is very difficult to examine, for example, non-verbal abilities in relation to those expected for a child of a particular age, without using norm-referenced, standardised tests. How many psychologists could, for example, say whether a four year old child assembling a particular fifteen piece jigsaw, was showing above average, below average or average skills for their age?

However tests such as the WISC(R) (Wechsler, 1974) which are widely used with the general population are of little use in assessing the abilities of the language handicapped child. Typically such tests include both verbal and 'non-verbal' scales. Verbal sub-tests typically include extensive tests of vocabulary, tests of language comprehension and tests of expressive language. Clearly the language handicapped child will have great difficulty with such items. Psychologists must not conclude that a preschool child has a global learning difficulty on the basis of results on an inappropriate test, or on the basis of inadequate assessment.

Donaldson (1991) suggests that tests such as the WISC(R), which have separate verbal and non-verbal scales, provide a useful means of comparing children's linguistic ability with other areas of their intellectual ability. However the performance section of the WISC(R) is not truly a non-verbal test. While the child may not be asked for any verbal response in a typical task, such as arranging pictures in a sequence, she may have to follow quite complex verbal instructions in order to understand the requirements of the task. Psychologists specialising in language handicap have tended to turn to lesser known, and often very expensive, intelligence tests. However, close examination of some of these tests reveals major flaws. For example, although the Leiter International Scale (Leiter, 1947) has very attractive, easy to use materials and is based on visual matching tasks with no verbal instructions necessary, the normative data on which scores depend was drawn from a small, non-European population in 1947, making the resulting scores of very limited use. In Lothian Region it is recommended that psychologists use the Snijders-Oomen Non-Verbal Intelligence Test (SON) (Snijders and Oomen, 1976) as a measure of cognitive ability in young language handicapped children. This is a Dutch test, which has norms for both hearing and deaf children, tests a range of non-verbal skills and which can be administered entirely through mime and demonstration.

It has to be said that administering a SON to a preschool child with a language handicap can be a nightmare. As the test is not often used by most psychologists, unfamiliarity with the test protocols may make it necessary to refer to the handbook while testing. The test materials are poorly laid out in a variety of indistinguishable folders and are held in clinging, tight, plastic envelopes. Many preschoolers with learning difficulties, indeed many preschoolers, have limited concentration spans. Trying to maintain rapport while attempting to read a rather poorly printed handbook and prise pieces of jigsaw out of their containers is not an easy task. At the end of an assessment the psychologist may find himself surrounded by what looks more like a pile of junk than hundreds of pounds worth of psychometric assessment material. However, it is frequently very striking that in spite of these difficulties a child with a language handicap, who may have appeared restless, unco-operative and unable to concentrate when given verbal tests, often performs happily and concentrates well when given non-verbal tests within their competence.

Norm referenced IQ tests are, of course, only a part of a psychological assessment. Information needs to be gathered from parents in a structured way. There are many checklists which help in the collection of information about language skills and general development. Informal parental reports of language use, developmental history and so on, are of obvious importance. The Symbolic Play Test (Lowe and Costello, 1976) is useful with very young children, given the association between symbolic play and the development of language and cognition. This test has the added advantage, in contrast to the SON, of being exceptionally easy to administer and score and is often used as an ice-breaker with small children.

In most cases the psychologist will have test results available from a speech therapist which will provide details of language skills – expressive language, comprehension, vocabulary, grammar and so on. In situations where such information is not available the psychologist may wish to use anything from a simple test of receptive vocabulary, such as the BPVS (Dunn and Dunn, 1982) to a comprehensive battery of language assessment tests. Assuming that the psychologist does have speech therapy information, the most useful contribution to the actual assessment of language may be in observing the child in naturalistic settings such as home or nursery. Many speech therapy assessments are clinic based and, particularly in the case of pragmatic difficulties, this is not an ideal setting to assess the child's difficulties with language in real life settings. In practice the basic language assessment of preschool children with severe speech and language difficulties may be very straightforward. If, say, a four year old has only a small stock of words, which are rarely comprehensible to strangers and are seldom used in more than two word combinations, it is fairly clear that she has a speech and language difficulty.

The above brief outline of what might be called diagnostic assessment makes the process seem quite straightforward. One simply establishes that the child in question has speech and language skills which are very poor for their age, measures non-verbal ability and, if there is a marked discrepancy between language and general ability, concludes that the child has a specific language problem. There are, however, a number of problems. There is no clear agreement about how delayed language should be to constitute a 'handicap'. The relevance of intellectual assessment in delineating a separate category of difficulty is in doubt as many academics would suggest that cognitive factors have a fairly indirect effect on language development. Even putting aside these points, the idea that all children with speech and language difficulties will have a neat verbal/non-verbal skills discrepancy is not always valid. Many children with articulation or phonological difficulties have more widespread problems with co-ordination or motor planning. These difficulties may well give rise to a depressed performance on perceptual or non-verbal tasks. As Crystal (1984) pointed out, the last thing that many specific learning difficulties are is specific. They are frequently pervasive and may involve social, behavioural, motor and perceptual skills. Distinguishing between a child who is 'globally delayed' and a child who has a pervasive 'specific' disability is difficult both philosophically and practically. It is therefore important not to look blindly at test scores but to examine the child's whole range of abilities for evidence of possible areas of strength. Children with 'semantic-pragmatic' difficulties or autism may, in some cases, produce better scores on verbal intelligence tests than on non-verbal tests. Such children may have little difficulty in coping with the fairly structured, unambiguous verbal psychometric test item but may, for reasons of motivation or because, perhaps, of some associated neurological difficulty, find non-verbal tests problematic. By definition semantic difficulties are related to the use of language in real life situations and are best assessed through observation in the home and nursery and by reports from family members and teachers who know the child well.

Assessment in the classroom

The kind of diagnostic assessments outlined above are useful in forming an impression of the kind of difficulties a child may be experiencing and working out broadly what kind of educational programme and environment may be most useful for a child. It is clear, however, that psychometric tests, in particular, are of little use in working out what should be taught to a child. Curriculum related, criterion referenced assessment is more important in this area. One example might be the assessment of reading for a child in a language unit. In this situation the psychologist would be looking at exactly the same things with a language handicapped child as with any other child and would be attempting to produce a profile of skills. What is the child's conscious knowledge of phonology in terms of the ability to detect rhyme and alliteration? Can the child identify letters? Can he blend letter sounds into words? Is he aware of right to left sequencing conventions? Does he understand the message in a story? Does he make use of contextual cues? How do his skills in various areas compare with the expectations in the 5-14 English Language curriculum document (SOED, 1991)? Having gathered this information it is obviously the case that there will be a process of relating any difficulties to the child's difficulties with spoken language. However, the actual assessment of reading will be carried out in terms of identifying the child's skills and strategies rather than comparing ability with that of other children.

In the same way behaviour problems would be analysed in terms of seeking a strategy for their amelioration rather than ranking them for degree of severity.

If a language handicapped child persistently hits other children, then a behavioural analysis of the problem in terms of antecedents and consequences is likely to be of more help than an attempt to give the child an 'acting out' score, or place them at some point on a continuum of 'hostility'.

Integration, placement and assessment

It is interesting to note that while there is a general move in many local education authorities to integrate increasing numbers of children with special educational needs, the process appears to be acting in the opposite direction with children with language handicaps. It is certainly the case, in Lothian at least, that the increased number of places in special language units represents one of the few current areas of growth in special education. However, it is the policy of Lothian Region Education Committee that all pupils with special educational needs will receive the widest possible opportunity to have these needs met within a mainstream school. It is necessary, therefore, to consider mainstream placement when the assessment of a pupil's special educational needs has been undertaken at the multidisciplinary level outlined earlier.

The psychological diagnostic assessments, combined with assessments by other professionals, may establish that a child has special educational needs and that these are related to a specific language difficulty. For example one might identify a four and a half year old child with limited verbal comprehension, poor articulation, prone to tantrums on frustration, with a limited concentration span, social difficulties and poor hand control. The child's parents and the professionals involved may agree that these difficulties could not be dealt with adequately by an unsupported placement in a mainstream primary class with some input from the local community speech therapist.

In terms of special educational needs it might be felt that the child will need small group and individual work on basic mathematical and literacy skills and on communication and language skills; a consistent programme of behavioural management; and speech therapy, on an individual basis, several times a week, with liaison between the speech therapist and the class teacher.

However, in theory, such needs could be met in a local school, given a sufficient allocation of additional teaching time and speech therapy time. There is little evidence for a unique curricular approach in language units, although there is obviously an emphasis on language stimulation. The survey cited by Donaldson (1991) found that staff in language units broadly agreed that the approaches which were most helpful to children's communication development were games and free play, real life situations and child centred approaches encouraging spontaneous child initiated communication. Such activities are similar to those carried out by most mainstream primary teachers in their attempts to foster language development. The books, text-books and materials used in language units are widely used in mainstream schools. It may not, therefore, follow directly from an assessment indicating that a child has a severe specific language difficulty that she should attend a language unit.

In reality, however, the resource implications and practical difficulties of providing sufficient support and expertise in a local mainstream school make such placements problematic. Most local education authorities have tried to resolve the conflicting needs for high levels of cost effective support and the aspiration to keep children with special needs in close touch with mainstream school by placing language handicapped children in mainstream school-based units. Generally children attending such units have had little educational integration into mainstream classes and have only mixed with their peers at breaks and lunchtimes. Staff at language units are, however, increasingly making efforts to involve their pupils in appropriate mainstream class groups for academic subjects as well as social and aesthetic subjects. In this way the clear distinction between a place in mainstream school and a place in a special unit may become blurred to the point at which there is little difference between a heavily supported mainstream place and a language unit place, other than the regrettable separation of language unit attenders from their local neighbours and friends.

While I may have laboured this point it is important to remember that the fundamental aim of an educational psychologist's assessment is not to assign a child to a particular category of handicap but to identify the child's needs and to recommend ways in which such needs may be best met. It, therefore, does not necessarily follow that because a child has a severe specific language handicap that his needs will be best met in a unit for children with specific language handicaps. Equally it could be argued that many children with special needs might benefit from the small group and individual teaching, and speech and language therapy, in a semi-integrated setting, which is available in many language units.

This leads on to a final issue. Specific speech and language handicap is a relatively acceptable label to many parents, and language units are relatively acceptable placements. Like 'dyslexia', specific language handicap is a 'diagnosis' which is actively sought by some parents. Such a diagnosis holds out hope for the future and the prospect of a fairly non-stigmatising placement among children with relatively mild handicaps. Understandably some parents who have children with speech and language delays see such delays as their children's primary handicap and are reluctant to accept an alternative view; for example that their child has global learning difficulties which will require long-term curricular adaptations and small group teaching. In the face of what may sometimes be fierce parental pressure it is important that psychologists have a clear idea of the relevant and objective assessment procedures which are necessary to identify children with specific language handicaps. It is equally important to remember that language units are set up with the clear aim of improving a child's linguistic skills in an educational setting to enable the accessing of a broadly mainstream educational curriculum. Such a setting may be inappropriate for a child who requires a curriculum emphasising the acquisition of, for example, basic self help skills.

In this chapter it has only been possible to touch briefly on various issues relating to the educational psychologist's work with language handicap and I have concentrated largely on initial assessment and placement. Much work remains to be done to clarify theoretical ideas, improve assessment, evaluate different forms of intervention, assess teacher behaviour, improve teaching materials and consider curricular priorities. Bearing in mind, however, that when I started work as an educational psychologist, there was no real recognition of the educational difficulties faced by children with speech and language handicaps and no local provision available to meet their needs, there has been considerable progress in recent years.

References

Aarons, M. and Gittens, T. (1992) *The Autistic Continuum.* Windsor, NFER Nelson

Berger, M. (1987) *What is a Language Disorder? Proceedings of the First International Symposium on Specific Speech and Language Disorders in Children.* Reading, AFASIC/ University of Reading

Bishop, D. and Edmundson, A. (1987) Language-impaired 4 year olds. *Hearing Disorders,* **52**, 156-173

Crystal, D. (1984) *Linguistic Encounters with Language Handicap.* Oxford, Blackwell

Donaldson, M. (1991) *Children with Language and Communication Disorders.* Edinburgh, Scottish Office Education Department

Dunn, L.M. and Dunn, L.M. (1982) *British Picture Vocabulary Scale.* Windsor, NFER Nelson

Elliot, C.D., Murray, O.J. and Pearson, L.S. (1978) *British Ability Scales.* Windsor, NFER Nelson

Ingram, D. (1987) Categories of phonological disorder. *Proceedings of the First International Symposium of Specific Speech and Language Disorders in Children.* Reading, AFASIC/University of Reading

Leiter, R. (1947) *Leiter International Performance Scale Battery for Children.* Windsor, NFER Nelson

Lowe, M. and Costello, A.J. (1976) *The Symbolic Play Test.* Windsor, NFER Nelson

McTear, M. and Conti-Ramsden, G. (1992) *Pragmatic Disability in Children.* London, Whurr

Rutter, M. (1978) Diagnosis and definition of autism. *Journal of Autism and Childhood Schizophrenia.* **8**, 139

Scottish Office Education Department. (1991) *Curriculum and Assessment in Scotland. National Guidelines: English Language 5-14.* Edinburgh, HMSO

Snijders, J. and Snijders-Oomen, N. (1976) *Snijders-Oomen Non-verbal Intelligence Scale*. Haarlem, H.D. Tjeenk Willink

Wechsler, D. (1974) *Wechsler Intelligence Scale for Children (Revised)*. New York, The Psychological Corporation

Wing, L. (1988) *The Continuum of Autistic Characteristics*. Plenum

Young, P. and Tyre, C. (1983) *Dyslexia or Illiteracy*. Milton Keynes, Open University Press

Support for Learning for Language Impaired Children

Anne C. Macdonald

The phrase 'support for learning' has caught the imagination in education circles. It is conceptualised as a framework in which special needs in education are thought about, provided for and delivered to children and young people. This chapter is an attempt to unpack the philosophical ideas in the phrase 'support for learning', and then to see how they have worked out in practical terms in a peripatetic language unit support service in Tayside.

The idea of support for learning is as old as civilised culture itself. As any study in social anthropology will confirm, (e.g. Mead, 1955) people from diverse human cultures transmit their belief and value systems, their language and their learning to their young in socially consistent ways. Vygotsky (1978) documents this universally found social interaction as the basis for all learning. Wood (1980) usefully uses the term 'scaffolding' to denote this process. It describes the natural and homespun way of learning whereby it is viewed as a task, whose goals are jointly set by tutor and tutee. Task management strategies vary with the complexity of the task and the competence of the tutee. Three strategies or stages can usually be observed. Firstly sub-goals are set as the tutor structures the activity so that the tutee can manage as much of the task as possible with independence. Effective learning takes place in the second stage of the activity. During this phase the tutee needs support which is targeted to be just enough to allow the tutee to display emergent competences and skills. The resulting scaffold supports the learner and is dismantled bit by bit as the tutee is enabled to take over increasing responsibility for achieving the task sub-goals. The third phase is task completion. By this time the tutee may well have to assume full responsibility for finishing the task. The characteristics of this approach are joint ownership of the activity and clearly defined goals, set in a social context.

Learning support systems in schools are now broadly based on the Vygotskian tradition of partnership and support in learning, within a social context which reflects the learner's own cultural norms. When the phrase is applied to individuals with special needs in education, we are required to examine the appropriateness to learning of the social context we provide for them. In addition, it has come to include the rights of those individuals to an education in which they are active participants and set in an educational context whose social features include at least a measure of integration with normally functioning individuals.

The key elements of the support for learning concept are the empowerment and enablement of the individual. By empowerment is meant that the individual's rights are secured, by advocacy if necessary. Especially important, is the right to participate in society freely and without prejudice. By enablement is meant that positive steps are taken to ensure that the individual will be equipped to function as freely and as independently as possible in an integrated society. Both of these elements have profound implications for the ways education is planned and delivered to children and young people with special needs in education. They also raise fundamental questions. The right to integration in mainstream is seldom challenged these days, but does this right ever conflict with another set of rights which children have, namely the right to literacy (UN, 1980 in Young and Tyre, 1983) and, with it, oracy and numeracy?

Underpinning this philosophy is the individual's right to equality of opportunity. What this ought to mean for individuals with special needs in education is that the services they are provided with should open up to them the possibility of a meaningful degree of integration in society. Too often in the past, the educational services have been instrumental in segregating our society. Indeed the sociological perspective on schooling makes clear that education continues to be the means of social control (Tomlinson, 1982). However, a new wind of change is blowing through schools in the direction of more and more integration into mainstream of children with special needs in education.

The rest of this paper relates one attempt by Tayside Region to bring together the rights of special needs children to an education which accesses mainstream and which also enables and empowers them to function there, fully, freely and without prejudice. It describes the relationship of a language unit set in a mainstream primary school to the associated peripatetic outreach service to language impaired children in other mainstream schools. Close attention will be paid to the peripatetic service but the language unit is the starting point for the examination.

Language units in Scotland were the subject of a survey by a Working Party of Scottish Principal Educational Psychologists (1988). More recently the SOED has been gathering information on the services local authorities provide for language impaired children. Malloy (1989) carried out an evaluation of a peripatetic service to language impaired children. Her analysis centred round the perceptions of the support teachers, the class teacher and the pupil. A similar approach will be used in this paper. The language unit under consideration is in Dundee, and is an integral part of Fintry Primary School in whose classes children with language impairment of varying degrees spend some time in activities of a social and curricular nature appropriate to their needs. It is known locally, and in the remainder of this paper, as FLU. It has a well accredited history of consultancy and support to other schools who may have children who are experiencing some language impairment, through its peripatetic arm, FLUPSS (Fintry Language Unit Peripatetic Support Service).

In addition to the educational aims of the host school in which it functions FLU has one important specialist objective. Its one specialist aim is the full and final integration of its pupils into their neighbourhood school where they can be educationally managed within the range of support services available there. The success rate in achieving this aim over the last decade is undeniable. Only a handful of children out of 50 leavers have transferred into the special school; 80% have transferred into mainstream primary or secondary, with 20% transferring into support units at secondary school or into the special school.

During the FLU phase of a child's educational experience specialist teaching and therapy are holistic and delivered within an individual needs framework. Teaching and therapy are strategically targeted to make efficient use of a scarce resource. Such a targeted approach firstly facilitates the development of communicative competence and secondly ensures that the mainstream curriculum is brought within the grasp of the child. Thirdly it offers a balance between the child's right to those learning experiences appropriate to an integrated setting and the child's right to acquire on an individual basis those core curricular skills without which access to long-term, meaningful mainstream integration would remain limited. In addressing needs, attention is inevitably paid to the development of positive self image and esteem. This phase usually reaches its climax with the realisation that the child's needs are now of such a nature that they could be met in the neighbourhood school of the parent's choice. The phase culminates with a short period of negotiation during which all interested agencies contribute to a transfer case conference.

The class teacher's perspective

While the willingness to accept in mainstream children who have experienced major communication difficulties has been found to be generally favourable (Malloy, 1989) many mainstream teachers do express the anxiety that they may not be able to cope. We will explore their concerns under three headings: professional, curricular and philosophical concerns.

Professional concerns

These are anxieties which centre around teachers' professional perceptions of themselves and their often quite limited access to additional training. Concerns are often voiced that teachers are inadequately trained in specialist areas of individual need. Only a few will ever have had the opportunity to gain hands-on experience of children with special needs in education. In addition, children with speech, language or communication difficulties tend to be perceived as a group whose needs are such that they call for a high degree of professional specialism beyond what most mainstream teachers will have acquired through either training or experience. Mainstream teachers sometimes believe that children with special needs in education will be difficult to manage both educationally and behaviourally.

Curricular concerns
These anxieties relate to the additional planning and management involved in delivering an extended curriculum to children with special needs in education. It is argued that children who have needed an individually styled approach to facilitate learning will fail to progress at the same rate in mainstream since access to individual teaching there will be very limited. Concerns are also voiced that the curriculum offered in mainstream may not be differentiated enough to allow children with special needs in education to gain at the same pace as they have done in FLU.

Philosophical concerns
These are anxieties which are raised in questions about whether or not it is fair to integrate children with special needs in education right into the fabric of mainstream interaction with all its flaws and imperfections. There is probably universal agreement that integration is right in principle. What is being questioned is whether it is good for the child. Behind these essentially moral concerns for the child with special needs is sometimes the concern that the addition of such a child may result in a diminution in attention paid to the needs of other children already in the class.

The child's perspective

The children themselves exchange the security of FLU and the peer relationships they have made during host school integrational experiences for the hurley-burly of full-time mainstream. In doing so, they face a transitional period of adjustment. Change is a major stress and we will consider three potential difficulties encountered by the child. These are emotional, social and intellectual difficulties.

Emotional difficulties
Stress caused by unmanaged, unplanned change can cause children to regress. Even with careful planning, however, the child will have to make adjustments to its own reference points. For instance, the self image which has been established in FLU will have been made with reference to the dominant peer group there. In a different peer group this self image of the child may suddenly undergo a distortion with the realisation of the creation of a new pecking order over which there is no control. While the 'freshman' child searches for new reference points,

the new peer group will be active in making their own sense of the newcomer. One of the easiest ways of doing this is by stereotyping. To anyone with SEN connections, stereotyping represents a major threat to self esteem. Excesses of labelling, name calling and patronising may result from stereotyping and these can be potentially damaging to the self image.

Social difficulties
Social difficulties arising from emotional stress have already been hinted at. Additionally however, the language-impaired child will face further social difficulties due to the impact of communication dysfunction on social functioning. New friendship bonds are not easy to forge in established peer groups even for children with average communicative skills. Children whose communicative competence is poor are among the most vulnerable in a social order where chat, planning, scheming, joking and gossiping are valued skills. Social difficulties may not be easily spotted since much social exchange will take place when the teacher is not present, at lunch breaks or intervals. Undetected difficulties with the social milieu may lead to fragile emotional states.

Intellectual difficulties
Although these difficulties cover every aspect of learning, from new routine learning to academic learning, it is the difficulties created by an academic framework to the curriculum which have most serious consequences. Whether 5-14, Standard Grade or SCOTVEC, the mainstream curriculum will be assessment orientated in a public way and to a degree not encountered before. The curricular framework is built around the need to assess progress. Levels, grades, objectives attained, invariably include measurement which sooner or later will use the language of comparison. While children with special needs in education will probably progress at an enhanced pace as an effect of planned and managed mainstream following FLU placement, they may despite their efforts and those of their teachers, conceive assessment related anxieties. These are based on the perception that intellectual status is quantifiable apart from effort. While this process as such does not give children intellectual difficulties, it defines for them that they have intellectual difficulties.

The Fintry Language Unit Peripatetic Support Service

FLUPSS was set up in response to these concerns, in order to meet these identified mainstream needs. The need is for specialist support to assist in the full and final integration into local mainstream schooling of children with speech, language or communication difficulties. This service is guided by the principle that the local mainstream school is the manager of both the child and the teacher, and of their concerns. This principle is fundamental and prescribes the operation of FLUPSS. Arising from this principle are the ground rules of functioning:

- FLUPSS is an enabling agency;
- FLUPSS provides special support which is additional to the normal support services of the school;
- FLUPSS is a scaffold type support system.

FLUPSS as an enabling agency

By labelling services as specialist, the danger may be created that expertise belongs only to the specialist. This perception can easily result in the distancing of mainstream teachers from children with special needs in education. It may even work to de-skill class teachers in learning difficulty management in which they had believed themselves to be competent. By being aware of these dangers, the need is heightened for FLUPSS to have a distinctive enabling function. Methods of enabling class teachers have included specific PAT seminar type work; but consultative liaison on a regular basis is more characteristic.

FLUPSS will also be an enabling agency to the child. As a familiar and trusted person, the FLUPSS teacher will be in a good position to bolster the feel-good factor and self confidence of the child. This can be achieved in working with the child in a group along with other children at a task directed by the class teacher. It may mean working on an individual task with a specific planned objective with the child alone. It may mean taking another group in the class to allow the class teacher to work with the child. The ways of working are many and are the responsibility of the class teacher to manage. Its aim is always to enable the child to cope with the demands of the new learning environment.

FLUPSS seeks to enable the class teacher/s to manage their own concerns and those of the child during the period of FLUPSS attachment. At the end of the day, FLUPSS involvement must result in the dissemination to the mainstream school of such SEN information as relates to the relevant language impairment of the child. In this process the class teacher/s will be acquiring tutor skills and knowledge of how the language impaired child learns. To fail to grasp the enabling function of FLUPSS is to run the risk of attributing expertise only to specialists, thereby quashing any notion that class teachers may learn new skills.

FLUPSS as additionality

FLUPSS input in a school is to be seen as support over and above what is normally available in mainstream schools in the way of support for learning systems. FLUPSS is not an alternative to learning support, but is both supplementary and complementary to it, by providing additional specific targeted support for a planned period. The aim of such support is to help the mainstream teacher to manage the child's needs and to help the child to settle emotionally and socially into a new environment at a time when stress is likely. It is not intended to be a permanent feature of the educational management of the child. In providing this service, recognition is made of the need for staff development created in mainstream teachers by the introduction into their classes of children with special needs in education. Recognition is also made of the needs of the child at a vulnerable transitional time. Since it is a scarce commodity, such additionality is subject to allocation by priority. It is also subject to continual review to ensure that it is meeting the objective set for it.

FLUPSS as a scaffold system
Reference has already been made to the temporary nature of FLUPSS. FLUPSS operates in a similar model to the Vygotskian support system. As we have already seen, the tutor creates a scaffold around the emerging skills of the learner and then removes the support bit by bit as the learner becomes more competent. The tutor delivers the exact measure of support needed to achieve the learners' goals. In the FLUPSS model, the learners are both the child and mainstream teacher. Thus the scaffold is around them both and dismantled as competence becomes established. More support during periods of 'blip' can be given, but only at the expense of other users, underlining the need to prioritise and hold the support arrangements under constant review.

We have looked at the relationship between FLU and FLUPSS, at the need for a peripatetic service to language impaired children, at its operating principle and ground rules of its working. I now propose to focus on four short case-studies to illustrate the practice of these principles.

The first case-study relates to the transfer from FLU of a speech and language impaired child at the P5/6 level into neighbourhood primary schooling. The second and third case-studies refer to the transfer into the first year of the same secondary school of two young people with a major communication dysfunction and other autistic attributes. The fourth case tells of the support given to a speech and language impaired child from nursery school through to P3 in a mainstream school. The child in the first case is female and is A, those in the second and third are B (male) and C (female). The mainstream child (D) is fourth and is male.

Case A

A came to FLU as a five year old with unintelligible speech and very delayed language, both apparently the result of an intermittent hearing loss at the crucial stage of phonological acquisition. She had a high sociability factor with good play and interactive skills, which due to her positive self esteem, were not dependent on competent speech and language. As in many children with communicative difficulties, she would often resort to nonverbal means of control. In common with most of them, she experienced delay in the onset of the P1 curriculum, and when during her first three years of schooling her literacy and numeracy skills started to emerge, it began to look as if the learning delay might be compounded by learning difficulties of a more endemic nature. However, she responded well to the FLU management of her speech, language and learning difficulties, so that by the end of her fifth year at FLU she was ready for transfer to a mainstream neighbourhood school. The normal liaison procedures took place and A was transferred after the summer break into a P5/6 class in a school whose balance tipped towards the more able child. FLUPSS involvement was for two half mornings. Over a one year period A's reading skills had increased by a year, her spelling and writing skills had risen from the stage of being able to write a single sentence with variable spelling, to written work of a paragraph's length with good spelling. Likewise her numeracy skills had increased from a P2 level of functioning to a P3 level. This is the story of a successful but fairly typical transfer.

Cases B and C

These are two autistic young people who came to FLU as six year olds from a special assessment preschool unit where a start had already been made to their social difficulties. A further difficulty for them is in understanding language beyond the literal, first order level and is a disabling factor for them in learning. Although B is more able socially than C, C is more able intellectually than B. The underlying difficulty for both of them in both areas of functioning is of an autistic nature. It is impossible to quantify in terms relative to alternative forms of schooling, the considerable social and intellectual progress they each made while at FLU. The pervasiveness of autism is such that these two young people remain autistic, but have been taught strategies to enable them to function in an integrated society. B and C transferred from FLU to a local secondary school at the end of their primary schooling. The secondary school was very positive about admitting B and C while raising understandable concerns that given the degree of impairment experienced by B and C, and due to the lack of opportunity for staff development, their school might not be the ideal placement. Both young people had the services of the learning support department of the school working with them in their classes in their first year. FLUPSS was able to supplement this with two further half mornings' attachment, allocated to the learning support department to manage. This arrangement gave B and C additional pastoral and academic help and provided for the operation of a consultative function within the secondary school. In addition FLUPSS led a PAT session at the school for some 25 teachers who wanted to know more about autism. The remainder of the secondary education of these two young people will be determined by the review process. The achievements of both children have been variable, with the case of B raising the concerns of some teachers that he is not gaining much intellectually from the placement. The school have responded to this challenge by timetabling him to receive some tuition on a withdrawal basis. The case of C has raised concerns about her sometimes quite bizarre behaviour which draws attention to her.

Case D

Case D is presented as an example of an attempt to manage a language impaired child in mainstream with FLUPSS assistance, but without a prior period of FLU placement. FLUPSS became involved with D once per week during the final year of his nursery schooling. His referral was based on the need of his teacher to have specialist input. Although he functioned well with the routine of the class and was highly sociable, his level of intelligibility presented a major problem for his teacher though not for him. At the end of his time in nursery school, peripatetic support into mainstream primary was requested, and given. At the end of his infant education in mainstream, he is mostly intelligible to the highly tuned ear of the peripatetic specialist, but not always to his class teacher. He has no difficulty socially, is well adjusted, happy and accepted by his peers. His comprehension is good while his language does remain delayed. Concerns are expressed at the level of his academic attainment which appears to represent an under achievement against his potential as measured by his comprehension. This is supported by the comparison of his attainment with that of a younger FLU pupil whom we shall refer to as E. E has similar speech and language difficulties to D, but has greater receptive language difficulties than D. In spite of a year's less schooling and greater problems with comprehension, E is at roughly the same emergent stage of reading as D, and is at the same stage of maths development.

Several factors can be identified in successful transfer from FLU to neighbourhood mainstream:

1. prior to transfer to full mainstream, the child receives help with communication difficulties in an educational setting which addresses them by offering intensive speech/language therapy integral with educational programmes;

2. prior to transfer to full mainstream the child acquires a basic level of oracy, literacy and numerical competence which allows the child to access mainstream learning at a level which can be managed during the transfer phase into mainstream and beyond;
3. positive feelings towards the child are found in the neighbourhood school;
4. during the period of FLUPSS involvement there is a marked attempt to enable the class teacher to fully manage the child.

Discussion

Once children are within the aegis of special educational provision, several factors can make it difficult for them to leave the sheltered setting for the rough and tumble of mainstream. These factors relate to the implication of small group teaching for learning. The major advantage of small group teaching lies in its responsiveness to need, and is therefore a clear choice for the education of children with special need. But this very advantage can be turned to disadvantage when individual needs are set out without reference to mainstream targets. A second disadvantage of small group teaching is that the learners are always being observed and watched. This creates dependency in the learner who may experience difficulty in learning in a larger group.

Teachers of children with special needs in education may also experience difficulty in making the decision to mainstream the child. It is argued (Tomlinson, 1982) that since their professional interests lie in the identification of special need, they have a vested interest in its maintenance. Many teachers both of mainstream and of special needs, still believe children to make better progress in separate provision with access to integration limited to social activities only.

Our finding, based on observation of cases such as A, B and C, and on comparison of cases such as D with E, shows that the unit enclave is a necessary provision for many children. It is necessary because it allows them to acquire the core skills of literacy and oracy to a level which makes the management of a literacy based curriculum possible for them by mainstream teachers. It is also necessary because it allows children with special needs to acquire the core skill of numeracy. The importance of numeracy to special needs individuals lies in the induction it gives them into hypothetico-deductive thinking. The distinctiveness of Western culture can be attributed to the influence on cognition of such rationality. Thus the acquisition of a mathematical understanding, even at a basic level, represents more than the accumulation of number facts. It provides the tools whereby youngsters can engage in problem-solving activities (SOED, 1991). It is the ability to problem solve, based on rationality, which will allow our youngsters to lead independent, integrated lives. By taking the route through the unit enclave, full, final functional integration within the range of support services available in mainstream ought to be a real possibility for a proportion of children with special needs by the time they reach puberty, the time at which such integration crucially matters to them.

This route is further justified and enhanced by the progress children appear to make after transfer into mainstream. We noted (see Case A) that there comes a point of preparedness, which in the interest of further progress, needs to be responded to by such transfer. This is because the gentle ethos of the unit will not provide enough challenge beyond a certain point of skill acquisition. Indeed it may mitigate against the kind of accelerated progress which we see after transfer. Mainstreaming at the right time can give a large boost to confidence and to learning. As part of the long-term plan in the management of special needs, the unit enclave is a necessary provision. On its own, however, the unit enclave can be an insufficient provision. FLUPSS bridges the gap between the necessary and the sufficient.

The value of FLUPSS and other specialist support services based on the same model is easy to define in a market orientated approach. It is demonstrated firstly in its efficiency in delivering continuity of experience between unit and mainstream. Secondly, by using existing resources to enable mainstream staff development, its value can be demonstrated in economic terms. Nowhere is the value of the model of specialist unit followed by specialist support in mainstream more clearly seen than in the cases of B and C. Considering that the long-term educational prognosis for them at the preschool stage was for a special school education or a residential placement, the fact that they have been enabled to manage in mainstream secondary must be indisputable evidence of the value of both unit provision and peripatetic specialist support.

While market forces are an inevitable part of the reality of education in the nineties, the driving force of innovation and change ought to be the effects of such intervention on the consumers rather than a focus on the cost. The consumers of FLUPSS are pupils and their mainstream teachers. The advantages to mainstream staff of specialist support systems are that they supplement mainstream with a degree of expertise, consultation and back up. There are clear advantages for the child who experiences a sense of community by belonging to the local school, feels supported at a time of stress and enjoys feelings of success in achieving mainstream targets. These observations are consistent with Malloy's findings.

Summary

Specialist support services of which FLUPSS is an example are a necessary investment in an education service which is committed to meeting the special needs of groups such as the hearing, the language and the visually impaired. They offset the hidden cost of integration by providing an effective, simple and economic means of staff development of mainstream teachers in these specialist areas. By doing so they make possible the full and final integration of youngsters with special needs in education. They are valuable services which are firmly rooted in the support for learning concept which itself has a long history in meeting the needs of society for continuity in the transfer of knowledge, skills and understanding from one generation to the next.

References

Malloy, I. (1989) 'An evaluation of a language unit'. Unpublished dissertation. Edinburgh, Moray House Institute of Education

Mead, M. and Wolfenstein, M. (1955) *Childhood in Contemporary Cultures*. Chicago, University of Chicago Press

Scottish Office Education Department. (1991) *Curriculum and Assessment in Scotland. National Guidelines: Mathematics 5–14*. Edinburgh, HMSO

Tomlinson, S. (1982) *A Sociology of Special Education*. London, Routledge and Kegan Paul

Vygotsky, L. (1978) *Mind in Society*. Cambridge, Massachusetts, Harvard University Press

Wood, D. (1990) Teaching the young child. In *The Social Foundations of Language and Thought,* ed. D. R. Olson. London, Norton

Working Party of Scottish Principal Educational Psychologists. (1988) *Children with Communication Difficulties*. Available from Dr J. Watson, Moray House Institute of Education, Edinburgh

Young, P. and Tyre, C. (1983) *Dyslexia or Illiteracy: Realising the Right to Read*. Milton Keynes, Open University Press

Phonological Indicators of Specific Language Difficulties

Dorothea Bogle

Introduction

Rutter has observed that one million school children in the UK aged between five and sixteen suffer from a communication disorder (1990). Of these, the vast majority do not have serious learning difficulties or physical disabilities but suffer from a hidden problem – confusion with language. That such children remain undetected early in their school experience is a sad indictment on the system, and has obvious implications for expense in effort and funding later in their career. Much more importantly, unless the children are picked up early and given appropriate support, their performance will continue to fall further behind those of their peers, with all the resultant traumas and feelings of failure that this inevitably will engender.

From the training point of view, as more children with learning difficulties are destined to become absorbed into mainstream schooling, it becomes increasingly urgent to equip teachers, health visitors and carers with the necessary skills to identify those likely to encounter literacy difficulties at a stage where prompt and appropriate action can help minimise their problems.

Recent evidence from researchers such as Snowling (1987, 1991) and Singleton (1988) strongly suggests that early difficulties in processing listening and speaking – the oracy skills – are important indicators of later problems with reading and writing. Although they do not require to be experts in this area, teachers, health visitors and other carers who are in constant touch with young children need to possess a solid background of understanding which will equip them both to identify children 'at risk' and to respond appropriately to worried parents. They already possess a 'craft knowledge' based on years of experience with small children, and few teachers, or indeed parents, entertain serious concerns without due cause. However, there is a requirement for more structured input which will allow teachers to make informed judgements about a child's performance, based upon an awareness of how language normally develops at preschool level. This will establish a base line upon which to develop their own understanding of possible deviations from the norms. At the early stages of language development, the graph of the language-impaired child's achievement will not diverge too far from that of his peers. However, if no help is offered, the lines of development will grow increasingly far apart and more work will be required at later stages with less hope of success. Unless the learning takes place at the crucial milestones of linguistic development when the child is ready to make the links and understand the concepts involved, the graph seems to slow down. Perhaps this is in part due to a sense of failure and a growing lack of self-confidence in their ability to succeed.

The processes of language acquisition are complex. The causes of language disorders are even more complex. Researchers uncover more layers in the puzzle, and more parameters need to be considered. External factors play an important role in the developing linguistic system. Emotional traumas within the family can cause severe disruptions and the child may stay on a plateau or even regress. An event as natural as a new baby in the family may lead an elder sibling to regress to more immature forms, perhaps as an attention-seeking device. Language deprivation in early childhood with the absence of close emotional bonding, and the attendant verbal and non-verbal interaction, may have long-term effects as the child has been deprived of the crucial listening phase during which he internalises the patterning of the mother-tongue. For present purposes, however, attention is focused on the verbal, post twelve month development.

Content of a teacher-training course

As a preliminary to any examination of language disorder, teachers require a framework of reference, and any teacher-training course needs to start with an examination of normal language development. An awareness of normal patterns of acquisition will also suggest fruitful lines for future programme planning. All children pass through similar general patterns although at varying paces, and the slow learner needs to be guided through the milestones, moving forward more gradually, and with regular rehearsal and recycling opportunities.

Guidelines on normal language development are laid out in an accessible form in Webster and McConnell (1987), and short checklists or 'profiles' are provided at the back of the text for assessments at the ages of two, three and a half, and preschool. It is advisable to approach any lists of 'normal performance' with caution as wide variations are to be expected. (Even researchers vary in their opinion of what is 'normal' and the average number of words in the vocabulary for a two year old has been variously reported as anything from two hundred to four hundred!) It is nevertheless useful to have starter reference-points, even if these simply act as sounding-boards for one's own impressions.

Recent researchers such as Snowling (1987) and Bradley et al. (1990) have highlighted the role played by phonological acquisition, the development of the sound system, as an early indicator of a child's general language competency. A well-developed phonological awareness is regarded as a positive ability which predicts successful performance in literacy skills at primary school. The child who enjoys rhymes and acquires the phonological features quickly and easily will be in a stronger position to cope with the requirements of reading and spelling.

An examination of the development of the consonants in the child's phonological system will serve as an illustration. Consonant acquisition provides a helpful indicator of articulatory age. Certain general patterns of development have been observed by researchers in the area (Anthony et al., 1971; Grunwell, 1987). In normal development:

1. the front consonants will appear before the back consonants, so that 't' and 'd' are established before 'k' and 'g':
   'Daddy tar' for 'Daddy's car'
   'Mummy done way' for 'Mummy's gone away'
2. the stops appear before the fricatives:
   'toder' for 'soldier' ('t' for 's')
   'pis' for 'fish' ('p' for 'f')
3. single consonants appear before clusters:
   'no' for 'snow'
   'gove' for 'glove'
4. 'w' appears before 'r' and 'l':
   'gwove' for 'glove'
   'twain' for 'train'
   'wowy' for 'lorry'
5. 's' appears before 'sh':
   'fis' for 'fish'
   'sops' for 'shops'
6. 'th' is the last consonant to be integrated into the system and versions such as 'fum' for 'thumb' and 'free' for 'three' are usual until six or seven years old.

Once some norms of development have been established, however flexibly, teacher-trainees are also in a position to describe performances which are immature but still following normal lines of development. For example, a child's chronological age might be four and a half years, but he may be performing like a three and a half year old in his articulation.

The child's performance must then be related to his chronological age. /pu:n/ for 'spoon' would be 'normal' for a three and a half year old, but immature for a four and a half year old. Provided that the child has no deafness caused by minimal hearing loss or 'glue ear', however, and can hear the difference between two sounds in minimal pairs such as 'sip' and 'ship', the assumption is that the usual maturational processes will alleviate early concern. It is unlikely that a child who is performing up to the level of his peers in all respects apart from articulatory immaturity will have longer-term problems at school age. Other isolated pockets of difficulty might affect word order, for example, and such features should be noted. The degree of severity and extent of any deviations seem to be the crucial factors in any consideration of long-term difficulty.

The question arises – *when should intervention be considered?* For example, if the child is four and a half years old and due to enter primary school at the next intake, and still lags seriously behind his peers in the phonological area, he may lack the sounds to relate to the letters. Teachers would then be concerned about this child's ability to cope with the requirements of reading and writing since he does not yet have the full framework of the sound system. Similarly, if a child's auditory memory does not allow him to link 'and' in 'hand' with 'and' in 'sand' or 'land', this will have serious implications for the transition to reading (Bradley and Bryant, 1990). As a rule of thumb, if a child's performance falls more than a year behind that of his peers, this constitutes reasonable cause for referral to a therapist.

In a case where the child is able in other areas of learning and has no obvious medical reason for problems with language, the label 'specific language difficulty' is usually applied. Snowling (1991) defines specific learning difficulties as 'unexpected difficulties which are out of line with a child's normal cognitive development'. The term 'dyslexia' is also used to describe those children whose performance falls below expectation in the written language. It affects the child's literacy development and, to a greater or lesser degree, his ability to access the curriculum. However, dyslexia is a wider problem than language alone and there will be other signals which point to the child's difficulty in information-processing. Singleton (1984) pinpoints the following as early indicators of this specific learning difficulty:

1. delayed onset of speech;
2. direction confusion (left/right);
3. handedness;
4. memory-related problems;
5. problems in sequencing;
6. motor dysfunctions.

From the linguistic point of view, a common factor observed by all recent researchers in the field of specific learning difficulties is weak phonological awareness. This inability to process the segmentation of words into syllables and to hold an auditory memory of speech sounds in the correct order results in problems with remembering words, retrieving them from the longer-term memory and sorting out the order of instructions. As mentioned above, impressive results have been obtained by Treiman (1987), Snowling (1991) and Bradley and Bryant (1990) which confirm the predictive relationship between a child's performance on phonological awareness tests and later aspects of their reading and written performance. Difficulties with sequencing, categorisation and memory obviously have serious implications for reading and writing and, if identified early, work can be started before they seriously affect school performance.

If we now examine the consonant development of children with suspected language disorder, this will show features which do not occur in the normal child of over three years of age. These may include:

1. confusions in voicing, with 'p' and 'b' confused in words such as 'boon' for 'spoon' and 'k' and 'g' confused in 'gar' for 'scarf';
2. confusions of nasals, with a preference for the bilabial 'm' ('keem' for 'queen', 'mife' for 'knife', 'nunk' for 'milk');
3. confusions of place of articulation consonants ('p' replaces 't' in 'pwins' for 'twins' and 'k' in 'mompy' for 'monkey');
4. omission of syllables in polysyllabic words ('bewa' for 'umbrella', 'emtin' for 'elephant'); most normal developers produce the correct number of syllables, although they may still have immature speech sounds (e.g. 'umbwewa'): among 510 preschool children tested in Edinburgh aged four and half years, only one child had the wrong number of syllables in 'elephant' and two in 'umbrella' (Anthony et al., 1971);
5. a tendency towards a syllable-timed rhythm, where each syllable is given equal stress and the ordinary syllable carries the beat ('birth 'day 'cake, 'lit'tle 'bun'nies).

Spoken English uses a stress-patterning where the stressed syllables carry the rhythm and therefore this atypical rhythm represents an important deviation from normal development. It is a difference which will also affect our reception of the language and our processing of meaning, as we tend to listen for the characteristic rhythmic groupings with stresses on the important content words in spoken English. Consequently, problems at the level of rhythm have implications for the receptive as well as the productive level. Both the rhythm of the mother-tongue and basic intonational contrasts are acquired in the first year of life and breakdowns in these features signal serious dysfunction in the child's ability to systematise what he hears into meaningful patterns. Children with atypical development are not consistent about their substitutions and therefore should be contrasted with those who use a slushy 's' and/or the uvular 'r' (Northumbrian burr) which, although they do not appear in normal development, do not lead to any communication breakdown as they are consistent substitutions. A feature of children with language 'disorder' (as opposed to 'delay') is more erratic patterning and a less predictable overall profile of performance.

It is probable that the articulatory patterns of these children will show immature characteristics as well as atypical features. There will be constant regressions to earlier forms, and they will acquire the new patterns more slowly.

Fig. 3.1

Age 4.0 years	Normal	Delayed	Disordered
bridge	bwidge	bidz	bit
train	twain	tain	daim
glove	gwove	gove	dub
clouds	cwouds	couds	poud

It is possible to postulate that the features that are showing up may in fact be extremely immature and protracted, rather than deviant patterns. However, until more research has been undertaken into the development of the phonological acquisition of the pre-two year old , this must remain a hypothetical consideration.

The point to make here is that this is a *specific* language difficulty. The child's performance in other areas may be up to or even exceed that of his peers. Many dyslexic children have well-developed visual skills for example. Children with these specific problems should be contrasted to children who are experiencing general delay in language. General language delay is consistent with an overall lower level of performance. The child who demonstrates severe articulatory delay is likely to show delays in other areas in language development as well (unless of course this is due to muscular inco-ordination associated with a condition such as dysarthria). A child who demonstrates general language delay may still be referring to himself as 'me', have a limited vocabulary and a short attention span. If a child has not attained the normal developmental milestones at four and a half, the rate of learning seems to slow down.

It is also important that teachers can gauge whether a child is having problems with coping at the receptive level or if this is purely an expressive problem. A central, receptive problem in processing language is more serious and will have implications for literacy. The language-disordered child may be unable to pick out meaningful groups of sounds (words) from the stream of connected speech. The same linguistic organising principles will operate in literacy and the child will encounter difficulty with sequencing and categorising the letters as well as the sounds (e.g. 'hospital' becomes 'splitho'). This child will have poor understanding of word-sequencing (grammar) and might say 'Me's not one got' meaning 'I've not got one'. The incoming message also becomes a meaningless jumble of sounds. At a deeper level, there will also be problems with understanding links and connections between ideas such as opposites, fields of related vocabulary, comparatives and superlatives. The problem of finding the appropriate word to suit the context will cause extreme difficulties and this is referred to by therapists as problems with semantic pragmatism. For example, the child might use the phrase 'the red round to eat' meaning 'tomato'. The expressive language of a child with comprehension difficulties will be the outward sign of a central dysfunction. Support is needed to lead the child through the process of making the connections overtly at first, and based in the child's immediate context. It might even involve taking the child's hand and actually leading them to switch on the cassette recorder.

Fig. 3.2

INPUT	**COMPREHENSION**	**OUTPUT**	
Hearing	Decoding Encoding	Spoken Language	phonology = sounds vocabulary = words grammar = structure and inflections
Receptive Language		*Expressive Language*	

Resource materials are available which will assist in checking upon a child's understanding. Ann Locke's *Living Language* (1985), for example, is a resource pack which provides the tools for checking receptive language and does not require special training to administer. It starts with simple instructions such as 'Find the dolly/teddy' and moves on to the more complex two-part instructions such as 'Put the teddy on the chair'. The pack provides materials to lead a child through a carefully graded series of tasks aimed at building up specific areas of weakness. It can be used as an 'ideas-bank' and offers important advice on the need for a structured programme, limiting the amount of new learning and the need for regular recycling in different contexts. Locke recommends that teachers should be on the alert for the appearance of new structures in spontaneous speech. This will indicate that the child has reached a conceptual stage where he is ready to internalise the rule-systems and will benefit from reinforcement through formal teaching. For example, once the form 'I goed home' is used spontaneously, or 'I founded this', these represent real steps forward in the child's conceptualisation. The irregular forms will come later, but the concept of signalling past action has been grasped.

A number of children with language disorders also suffer from difficulties with their motor skills. They are frequently labelled 'clumsy' or 'accident prone'. Problems may involve fine skills such as holding a pencil or gross skills such as kicking a ball. Singleton (1984) makes an interesting distinction between classic dyslexics who usually come from families with a positive history of language difficulties, and those who demonstrate language and co-ordination problems, where birth trauma or high temperatures in infancy may have affected development.

There seems to be a snowballing continuum of difficulties from mild to severe and from immature to disordered.

Fig. 3.3

Normal	Normal but immature (possibly only in pronunciation)	Severely immature (pronunciation and general language delay)	Language disorder (delayed onset, immaturities and atypical patterns, direction problems, sequencing confusion, poor concentration)	Language disorder and global problems of co-ordination
	delay		disorder	

Summary

Teachers need information that will allow them to make informed judgements about whether a difficulty is:

1.	discrete and well-defined: e.g. articulation only = immature	*or*	more general: articulation + limited vocabulary + grammatical delay (few structures, limited use of connectors)
2.	immature but normal = delayed	*or*	atypical and not in line with usual development = disordered
3.	expressive (production only)	*or*	receptive (central processing) + expressive
4.	language disorder only	*or*	language disorder + global difficulties

Additional indicators

Observations during data gathering in the MRC research project in the 1970s into children's language in the Department of Child Life and Health at the University of Edinburgh produced a high incidence of the following characteristics in children referred to the Royal Hospital for Sick Children Outpatient Department for speech therapy, many of which foreshadow findings in the 1990s.

1. A history of speech and language problems in the family.
2. A birth history of trauma such as a high forceps delivery which may have led to minimal damage in the language area of the brain.
3. An unusually high number of multiple births in the extended family unit (twins).
4. A history of cold and chest infections in the child at a crucial stage in the early years. This would have affected their listening skills as the patterning and structuring of the language was being internalised.
5. A higher proportion of boys than girls. Some writers claim boys outnumber girls by as many as 4:1.
6. Cross-laterality or ambidexterity in the family.

In themselves, none of the above need give cause for concern; however, if several show up in a child's profile, it might be wise to regard this child as potentially at risk as far as language development is concerned.

The role of the teacher

Due to the complexities of this area and the real need to 'get it right' at an early stage, teachers should be given some hands-on experience in a monitored environment to allow them to come to grips with analysing real cases. Consequently, case-studies should be provided which demonstrate the various problems under investigation. Any cues and signals which lead to detection should be talked through and discussed within peer groups to help teachers focus their awareness and build-up their confidence. Additional case-studies can then be used for individual members to work through and present findings in feedback sessions. Once teachers have been given time to build up their own detection skills, based on greater understanding of the possible areas at risk, they will feel in a stronger position to discuss individuals with speech and language therapists, and to counsel the parents who are understandably anxious. It is important that the teacher should see herself as part of a team and be clear about the complementary roles played by the other members of that team.

The speech and language therapist acts as the expert who is in a position to identify the difficulty and to provide appropriate focused practice at regular intervals. As Edmonstone (1991) observes: 'There is still a place for individual therapy, but this can only be effective where a key-worker from the classroom is involved, so that the key-worker can continue the therapy at times when the therapist is not available'. Teachers are in a position to recycle learning points introduced during the therapy sessions and link them to real classroom practice. It is crucial to understand how to exploit usual classroom activities to respond to a child's need to extend vocabulary, to reinforce certain structures or to build up awareness of rhythm through songs and poems. The informed teacher is the 'key-worker' who can work alongside the speech and language therapist to develop learning-strategies and to move the child on to the next stage in linguistic development, making the links which the child has been unable to build on his own.

The teacher is also in a strong position to liaise with the family and encourage more parental involvement in the child's successful learning process. A loose-leaf file of activities to keep the family appraised of the child's progress is recommended by Arrowsmith (1992). This will provide additional opportunities for 'overlearning' of teaching points and will help to increase the child's confidence by encouraging him to believe that he can cope. It will also ensure that the programme is restricted to certain points only and the child is not moved forward too rapidly or required to tackle vocabulary which has not yet been introduced to the core programme. Discussion of goals and progress should invariably involve the parents, and supportive parents can provide valuable opportunities to extend the work already instigated by the therapist and picked up by the classroom teacher. The aim should be to foster a team approach which places the child's successful and confident progress at the centre, guiding decisions and planning development.

Where do we go from here?

Attempts to identify a child's strengths and weaknesses ('capacities' and 'deficits' in Snowling's terminology) will provide indications about the sort of materials and activities best suited to the individual needs. If the child has well-developed visual and semantic skills and is good at remembering the word pattern, or at guessing meaning from context, the teacher can capitalise on these strengths and draw overt links to counter weak phonological awareness. Any successful programme needs to be:

- **Tailor-made** to the individual child, as each child will present with a different complex of capacities and deficits within his own unique social and emotional context.
- **Structured**, leading the child to draw links and internalise new learning. Many children with learning difficulties suffer from poor organisational skills and care in planning their input is essential.

- **Sequenced** so as to recycle old learning and gradually build in the new thereby ensuring the child's confidence in his ability to succeed.
- **Learner-centred** and not teacher-dominated, with the child's contributions valued and his opinions discussed and developed.
- **Appropriate** to the child's ability level and chronological age.
- **Meaningful** and authentic in terms of materials used and tasks set.
- **Linked** to the child's routines.
- **Built upon the child's need to communicate.** The best content for a programme is interactive talk while engaged in a task. Conversation is the natural mode and will allow opportunities to extend vocabulary, practise structures and move the child forward socially as well as cognitively.
- **Designed to encourage self-awareness and confidence within the group.** Other children may be involved at the later stages as peer-learning is often the most successful.

The good news here is that many of the tasks and strategies are already in place in the nursery school or lower primary. Successful classroom practice holds no surprises for the sensitive teacher and mother. However, it is helpful to stand back to reflect upon the underlying principles that guide our thinking. Parents intuitively simplify their language and repeat the message in a number of different ways to ensure understanding. Sentences are short; key words are repeated. Learning is in the 'here and now' with overt links to real objects then pictures. In the same way, learning for the child with a problem should be simplified and structured with a limitation both on the amount to be learnt and the environmental stimuli. The child who is easily distracted and has a poor concentration span needs to be carefully focused, especially at the early stages. Too much input will distract and confuse. Most importantly, teachers should guard against making assumptions that the child has understood. Only after successful recycling of the learning in a variety of contexts can we safely conclude that a point has been learnt. The teacher's language must be appropriate, the instructions clear and non-verbal clues should be used to reinforce meaning.

Once the guiding principles have been laid down, the next stage is to point the teachers in the direction of suitable tasks and materials which will provide the means to achieve longer-term goals. A detailed teaching/learning strategy needs to be in place as well as good general practice. Exploiting usual activities such as co-operating in making a scrap-book could give the opportunity for categorisation – zoo animals on one page and farm animals on another. Blowing bubbles in the bath could suggest new vocabulary items to extend the child's lexical store, and compare or contrast sizes/colours/shapes. Rehearsing their telephone number is an excellent 'digit span' test, and helps build auditory memory. Figure 3.4 outlines some sample activities and games which will build up the child's competencies whether they are delayed or disordered. Both groups will benefit from structured teaching at pre-school in preparation for a more successful acquisition of the literacy skills.

To aid phonological awareness, practise poems and songs to 'feel' the beat and the rhythm. Bradley's tests such as the same and different (hand, sand, mind) and rhyming words (play/day) will also help auditory discrimination. Build up

Fig. 3.4

ACTIVITY	METHODOLOGY	CONCEPTUAL	LANGUAGE
I went to market...	Real game, authentic context	Helps memory and sequencing	Rehearsing tenses and vocabulary items • 'I went...' • 'I bought...'
Find the difference	Pair-work, interactive	Questioning, narrows down the options; negotiation	• 'I can see a...' • 'Have you got a...?' • 'Where is the...?'
Category building (find all the...)	Group-work	Finding sets of similar items, categorising and organising	Vocabulary-building in different contexts
Rhymes	Fun	Auditory perception	Good for rhythm and stress; identifying the important stressed words
Hiding objects on a tray	Competitive; motivating	Visual memory practice	Produces lists of objects
Hunt the...	Mime the object the child must fnd (e.g. drum, hat)	Spatial awareness	Prepositions: behind, under
Festivals: Christmas and Easter	Authentic and meaningful	Valuing individual contributions; listening to others	Building appropriate vocabulary
Telling a story, e.g. The Little Red Hen	Integrate the language skills – listening and speaking (later also reading, writing)	Builds concentration	Listening and responding; each child has a finger puppet and must move it as required in the story

listening skills and allow children to play with sounds ('a rum, a tum'). Extend activities beyond language to listening to musical sounds, to the rain or to making animal noises.

Goswani and Bryant (1990) suggest that different types of auditory awareness relate to reading and spelling. Awareness of onset and rhyme is a first stage ability and precedes the acquisition of reading ('b' = onset, '-and' = rhyme in 'band'; 'cl' = onset, '-ouds' = rhyme in 'clouds'). Once the reading skills begin to be established, awareness of the individual sounds or phonemes affects the letter/ sound relationship and therefore the ability to spell correctly.

Time spent in listening to the child is essential because it provides evidence of the present level of achievement. This will act as the basis for forward-planning.

Recognising the problem and working upon it at the early pre-school stage avoids traumas later on. Able children often go undetected at primary school because they develop successful coping strategies which disguise their inabilities. For example, the child with poor phonological awareness but strong visual skills, remembers the word patterns and copes by guessing a word from appearance and context. Differences in performance among individual children will depend partly on the severity of their deficit, and partly on their ability to maximise their other capacities. Sometimes it is as late as secondary school level before children with specific learning difficulties are identified. At this stage the requirements of coping with a complex curriculum, organising homework and the pressures of exams put an added strain on the child who has been able to cope at the primary level.

Conclusion

It cannot be overstated that language is crucial for a child's inner development as well as for healthy social bonding and emotional stability. The child who is hampered by a communication disorder tends to become marginalised in our society and to suffer from a natural frustration and resentment. Unlike the deaf and the blind, these children all too frequently slip through the early-detection net. More research and investment is needed and, at a more practical level, an increase in the number of speech and language therapists working with better-informed teachers, health visitors and carers.

Informal soundings would suggest that recent years have seen a rise in the number of children with language disorders being reported in primary schools. While it would be gratifying to believe that this reflects a greater awareness of problems on the part of the teachers, perhaps there is a more sinister explanation. Many teachers consider that non-interactive pursuits such as watching television are having a serious effect on language development. It is an easy option for a busy parent but there can be little doubt that in his home context the child is being deprived of opportunities for building and developing performance through modelling and expanding at the early stages and in learning appropriacy and negotiation skills as he moves up the educational ladder.

Perhaps this is a new form of language deprivation and it is one which is widespread and invasive. It makes the need for an enriching language experience at school all the more urgent and we must have effective strategies in place. There is no quick solution. Programmes of ongoing support must be devised in response to the varied needs of our individual children. However, what could be more important and worthwhile for any dedicated teacher than to be instrumental in devising the means to prevent frustration and a sense of failure in our growing generation?

References

Anthony et al. (1971) *The Edinburgh Articulation Test.* Edinburgh, Churchill Livingstone

Arrowsmith, J. et al. (1992) Sharing action and evaluation: parents and staff working together in early education. In *Spotlight 37.* Edinburgh, Scottish Council for Research in Education

Bradley, L. (1980) *Assessing Reading Difficulties: Diagnostic, Remedial.* Berkshire, NFER Nelson

Bradley, L. and Bryant, P. (1990) *Children's Reading Problems.* Oxford, Blackwell

Edmonstone, A. (1991) A functional communication approach. In *Innovatory Practice and Severe Learning Difficulties*, ed. J. Watson. Edinburgh, Moray House Publications

Grunwell, P. (1987) *Clinical Phonology.* Chapman and Hall

Goswani, U. and Bryant, P. (1990) *Phonological Skills and Learning to Read.* Lawrence Erlbaum

Locke, A. (1985) *Living Language.* Berkshire, NFER Nelson

Rutter, M. (1990) *Breaking Down the Communication Barrier.* AFASIC

Singleton, C.H. (1994) A stitch in time. *Special Children.*

Snowling, M. (1987) *Dyslexia: A Developmental Cognitive Perspective.* Oxford, Basil Blackwell

Snowling, M. (1991) Developmental reading disorders. *Journal of Child Psychology and Psychiatry*

Treiman, R. (1987) On the relationship between phonological awareness and literacy. *Bulletin of Cognitive Psychology*, **7**

Webster, A. and McConnell, C. (1987) *Children with Speech and Language Difficulties.* Cassell

Writing Difficulties: causes and advice for remediation

Anne E. O'Hare

This chapter considers children with writing difficulties in the setting of otherwise normal learning potential. Such children may be expressing slower development in this area, which may be influenced by a family history of similar difficulties, or they may have lost some aspect of writing competence secondary to an insult to the brain. The writing difficulty can therefore be regarded as developmental or acquired (O'Hare and Brown, 1989).

Normal development of writing

The stages of writing acquisition can be broadly grouped into penmanship, spelling and syntax and composition. During the first stage of writing orthographic coding, fine motor function and orthographic motor integration occur, and difficulty in acquiring these skills interferes with the rapid automatic production of written language. At the second stage the writing process calls more upon verbal working memory and the ability to generate different units of written language such as the word and the sentence. Beyond this at the third stage cognitive processes such as planning, translating and revising text come into play. Many children are constrained at the first and second stage and this leads to higher level writing disabilities either because the child is directly constrained by the inability to produce letters and written words, or indirectly because an aversion to writing, due to early frustrations with the acquisition of this skill, leads to a reluctance to revise written work when composing larger pieces of text (Berninger and Rutber, 1992).

Most children who experience difficulty learning to write are detected by their classroom teachers. The latter are able to holistically assess that the child's speed and legibility is less than would be expected for their peer group. For research purposes there are quantified measures of handwriting which tend to concentrate on penmanship and spelling such as the copying task in the group diagnostic reading aptitude and achievement test. Girls have faster test penmanship than boys and this discrepancy persists until the end of secondary school and a similar picture is seen with regard to sentence length (Dutton, 1992).

Penmanship difficulties

Visual spatial problems

Once writing is a fully established skill, vision is primarily required to monitor the position of the writing on the lines and on the page and to allow the text to be read. The actual execution of the letters has become a subconscious act and relies on the brain having laid down a memory of movement which is known as kinaesthesis. Prior to this stage the motor skill of writing depends firstly upon visual monitoring. Visual perceptual difficulties are an uncommon cause of writing problems but nevertheless they do occur in certain groups of children such as those who were born very premature. In this situation the child experiences difficulties not only with writing but also with drawing and there are features within the child's writing which occur more commonly in this type of penmanship difficulty: the margins vary, the writing tends to slope diagonally across the page, lines run into one another, letters are omitted, the end of the line is misjudged so that the child runs out of the page in the middle of a word and there is poor spacing between the words. These difficulties have equal expression in copying, writing to dictation and original composition although often the greatest difficulty is seen in the copying exercise.

Co-ordination problems

Co-ordination can be regarded as the ability to accurately judge distance, force, speed and direction of movement. Abnormalities in this area can be seen in children with mild cerebral palsy who lack the fine neat adjustment of the hand required to write. Their letters may be a mixture of too small and too large, their writing speed may be slow, and involuntary movements may cause sudden unexpected jerks with angulations of the letters and blotching and drawing of the pen across existing script. These abnormalities of the writing are evident in copying, writing to dictation and composition. Often the pen is held insecurely in a dagger or abnormal tripod grip and it may slip through the fingers. Such children may well be able to spell correctly orally and their executive penmanship problems may be overcome by a typewriter or word processor.

Dyspraxic problems

Although dyspraxia and inco-ordination often co-exist it is possible to separate out the former in quite a number of children who experience difficulties learning to write. Praxis is the conceptualisation of movement, i.e. the ability to plan movement and therefore a dyspraxia relates to a relative inability to learn how to perform a motor skill when the child is compared with their peers. Fine motor skills are learned according to a strategy, in that the individual components are learned in isolation and then they are sequenced into the final skill. With practice there is a gradual increase in speed and in neatness of the skill until the skill becomes automatic or subconscious. During the same time the brain is laying down a motor memory for the skill and the ability to plan movement depends on these past memories and experiences. A child may show difficulties in the acquisition of motor learning which are out of step with their cognitive learning.

The dyspraxia may be isolated for writing or it may involve other hand skills such as cutting with scissors, using feeding utensils, tying shoe laces and using tools. Speech may also be affected with a slow development of articulation.

Children with dyspraxia may well be able to write the letters in isolation but when they have to synthesise letters into words they express their difficulties. This can affect writing both in copying, dictation and in spontaneous composition, but because of the demands placed on the child during composition their dyspraxic features may be more pronounced. The writing is slow and laborious and the child rapidly loses concentration. He writes something down and then monitors it by vision, not kinaesthetic memory, so that when he sees that it is wrong he crosses it out, so frequent corrections and crossings out are characteristic. The mistakes within the writing may appear to be careless, in the sense that letters will end up upside down and back to front within a word, when the child could write them satisfactorily as a single letter. As such the mistakes that the child makes are characteristically inconsistent and thus perplexing to both them and their teachers. Many of these children will learn to read satisfactorily and may have quite well developed oral spelling skills, but there are others in whom spelling problems co-occur with the dyspraxia and this type of writing difficulty is particularly intractable when it comes to remediation.

Many children with dyspraxia eventually acquire the skill of writing and often with quite good legibility as they move into secondary school. However, they remain disadvantaged because of their slow writing speed. Such a pattern may lead to them using a key board in the earlier stages of writing acquisition, then dispensing with this towards the upper end of primary school only to want to take up such a system again in secondary school because of the constraints placed on them by their poor writing speeds. A child with a dyspraxic writing problem therefore merits monitoring and review throughout their school career.

Spelling and syntactical problems

Ontogenetically writing is the last language skill to develop in the child and is preceded by language comprehension, speech and reading. It is therefore the abnormality which is likely to persist the longest in delayed development of language or to be lost most easily in acquired brain disease. A child who has brain damage acquired after the development of speech, reading and writing may show a persisting disorder of writing even after there has been an otherwise good recovery in other fields (Heacen, 1976).

Spelling is the production of a correct sequence of graphemes to correspond to a word of spoken speech as dictated by the rules of the particular language. It is therefore not surprising and is also understandable in terms of the layout of the brain that syntactical and spelling writing difficulties often follow a developmental speech delay. Mastery of spelling requires a high degree of linguistic competence (Frith, 1978) and is the last language skill to develop. Problems with spelling often persist throughout the child's school career.

The child's writing speed is slow and they have difficulty retrieving words from their spelling vocabulary. Words may be written in a slavishly phonetic way or according to dialect and very occasionally in the same way as the child speaks them with their immature speech. Complex graphemes such as 'ph', 'ch', 'sh' and 'th' cause particular difficulties. Spelling age is delayed on standardised tests and mirror writing adds confusion to what at first may appear an unintelligible muddle but which often has patterns. The child may have little idea of punctuation, phrase or sentence and spacing and they often cannot read what they have written although they could read the same passage in typed script. They can copy well but writing to dictation and spontaneous composition is poor with the child often restrained by their short, poorly constructed, simple sentences.

The learning of syntax in speech follows the development of the phonemic system and in the same way sentence construction follows the development of graphemic skills. In this respect it is more related to motor development than cognitive learning and a child may have an above average IQ but a very profound spelling/writing difficulty. Acquired brain damage which affects motor learning with lips, tongue and palate often affects motor learning for writing as the two areas of control in the brain are adjacent. A spelling difficulty may remain well after the abnormalities of spoken speech have cleared.

There is often a family history of reading and writing difficulties in first degree relatives, particularly males. In such families there appears to be a maturational delay in the left hemisphere of the brain. The left hemisphere is preferentially developed for language in the majority of individuals. Recent techniques in brain electrical activity mapping and regional blood flow have confirmed these associations.

Semantic (composition) problems

Speech and writing are the usual means by which we express ourselves in a language, and if they are faulty then an alternative communication system is required – e.g. using language to re-develop concepts, understand and compare these concepts, and reason. Those children who have a semantic writing difficulty (that is to say, they have problems with the understanding of meaning in language) often have broader learning difficulties. However there are some children in whom the problem with language is specific and affects semantic use in writing.

Remediation

Reduce anxiety

Children with writing difficulties often have low self esteem and morale and this may be exacerbated by their ineptitude at physical activities (McKinlay, 1978). The resultant anxiety may manifest itself through physical symptoms such as migraine, more obvious features such as panic in relation to certain lessons, behavioural problems such as deliberate provocative behaviour or through general restlessness and poor concentration in the classroom. This anxiety blocks further learning.

Circumvent the handicap

Naturally there is a tendency to concentrate on remediating the child's writing problem and therefore concentrating on this area, so that the child feels that there is a strong focus on things that he cannot do, as opposed to things that he can do. The child with a writing difficulty needs to have some way of putting his ideas down in some form of retrievable store. This can be by photostating the work of another child in the class, accepting taped responses and the use of a scribe or acquiring typewriter or word processor skills (Goad, 1977). Such an approach where the handicap is essentially bypassed places an emphasis on communication and this in itself may ultimately promote development in handwriting even though the child has largely circumvented the need to write.

Practise areas without disability

The child's morale will depend on his stimulation of learning in areas where he has no disability. It can be difficult in some children with penmanship problems to identify areas in the curriculum or on the sports field where they can legitimately excel. But wherever possible, areas where he can succeed should be highlighted. Naturally an understanding of the amount of effort that the child may need to put into a piece of writing in comparison to another child in the classroom, needs to be recognised, and the child should receive appropriate praise. A correct balance can be difficult to achieve as the children are aware if they are being praised over a piece of work that they can see compares badly to that of other children in the classroom. However something like computer work may be particularly appealing to such a child and allow them to develop skills above the level of some of their classmates.

Prepare a remedial programme

Unfortunately for some children the development of useful writing skills eludes them and this is particularly the case for children with severe dyspraxias. In these instances continuing to bypass the handicap with the use of a keyboard is the best way forward. However there is value for many children in continuing to practice penmanship and spelling in a way which respects the child's problems in these areas and does not have unachievable goals. Some children benefit from modification to pencil design to improve grip and the use of non-slip material on the desk or taping of the paper to the desk or the use of a right-angled board (Myers, 1992). In some instances targeting the motor difficulties with occupational therapy and physiotherapy is effective in some areas of dysfunction, although the evidence that this translates directly into greater writing competency is not strong (Humphries, 1992).

References

Berninger, V. W. and Rutbert, J. (1992) Relationship of finger function to beginning writing: application to diagnosis of writing disabilities. *Developmental Medicine and Child Neurology,* **34,** 198-215

Dutton, K. P. (1992) Writing under examination conditions: establishing a base line. *Handwriting Review,* 80-101

Frith, U. (1978) Spelling difficulties: annotation. *Journal of Psychology and Psycholinguistics,* **19,** 279-285

Goad, M. (1977) A picture approach to typewriting. *Special Education Forward Trends,* **4 (1),** 14-16

Heacen, H. (1976) Acquired aphasia in children and the ontogenesis of hemispheric functional specialisation. *Brain and Language,* **3,** 114-134

Humphries, T. et al. (1992) A comparison of the effectiveness of sensory integrative therapy and perceptual motor training in treating children with learning disabilities. *Journal of Developmental and Behavioural Paediatrics,* **13,** 31-40

James, W. H. (1992) The sex ratios of dyslexic children and their sibs. *Developmental Medicine and Child Neurology,* **34,** 530-533

McKinlay, I. (1978) Annotation: strategies for clumsy children. *Developmental Medicine and Child Neurology,* **20,** 494-501

Myers, P. W. (1992) How the sloping board assists pencil hold and writing action in young children. *Handwriting Review,* 20-22

O'Hare, A. E. and Brown, J. K. (1989) Childhood dysgraphia Part 1: an illustrated clinical classification. *Child Care Health and Development,* **15,** 79-104

Strategies for Intervention: goals, techniques and settings

Morag L. Donaldson and Jennifer Reid

Introduction

An important issue in working with children with any type of communication difficulty is how professionals and parents can most effectively enhance or improve the children's ability to communicate. To be effective, intervention strategies must be geared to the needs of the individual child and therefore must be closely integrated with thorough, ongoing assessment procedures. Few would disagree with this statement, although there is less agreement about exactly how information from diagnostic assessments should be translated into intervention strategies. For example, should the main aim be to develop a child's strengths so as to compensate for his weaknesses, or should the emphasis be on developing the skills in which he is weakest? Whatever the answer to this question, it is clear that the more general question of 'What is the best intervention strategy for language and communication disorders?' is highly unlikely to be answerable in such a simple form. Instead, we need to ask a series of more specific and more complex questions concerning the effectiveness of particular intervention techniques in achieving particular goals, for particular types of children, with particular types of disorders, in particular sets of circumstances. The following sections aim to illustrate the range of possible approaches to intervention for children with language and communication disorders and to consider some of the evidence which can be used in addressing questions of effectiveness. For a more detailed review, see Donaldson (1992).

Intervention strategies vary along several dimensions, including those corresponding to the following questions:

1. What should be taught or developed?
2. How should the intervention be carried out?
3. Where should the intervention take place?

In other words, there is variation in the goals of intervention, in the techniques used to achieve these goals, and in the settings where the intervention takes place.

Goals of intervention

An intervention will usually have a variety of goals, ranging from very general goals to more specific goals or objectives. Typically, goals are arrived at through assessment procedures which are rather different to those through which the initial diagnosis of a particular language or communication disorder was made. Assessment for the purposes of diagnosis will probably be made using norm-referenced, standardised tests, which involve comparing the child's performance with that of a representative sample of other (usually normally developing) children and the assignation of an age-equivalent or other standardised score. Such norm-referenced assessments are not usually sufficiently detailed or informative for the purposes of planning intervention. For this purpose, clinicians may turn to criterion-referenced procedures, in which the child's performance is compared to a more detailed set of criteria or goals. These are typically organised as developmentally-sequenced levels, and the child's abilities are matched to a developmental level or other standard, either through observation or through testing (which may be informal or standardised). Examples of assessments used for planning treatment would be the Detailed Test of Comprehension, from the Derbyshire Language Scheme (Knowles and Masidlover, 1982), which is an unstandardised test, and the Pragmatics Profile (Dewart and Summers, 1988), in which information on developmental level is gained through a structured interview with the child's parents or carers. Linguistic profiles (Crystal, 1982) are derived through the analysis of elicited speech samples, and these are used in particular by therapists working with children who have more complex and persisting impairments and who are receiving intensive remediation, for example, in a language unit.

Developmental goals are selected to help a child achieve those aspects of language which would be the next to appear according to some generally agreed developmental sequence, based on the literature on language development in normal children. This approach works rather better for those aspects of language about which there is a large literature, such as the acquisition of grammatical tense inflections, but can be problematic in areas about which less developmental information is available, such as the acquisition of conversational rules. In fact, developmental goals may not be particularly functionally relevant to a given child in her/his own circumstances. The selection of appropriate goals may therefore be influenced by functional considerations, so that the language skills acquired suit the individual needs of the child and are more likely to lead to pragmatic gains.

Although different types of intervention goals are far from mutually exclusive, there has been a historical shift away from an emphasis on the structure of language towards an emphasis on language as a tool for communication. The relative emphasis on these two types of goal also varies according to the nature of a child's language problems. For instance, for a child with a phonological-syntactic disorder, intervention is likely to focus on language form, although not in isolation from function, whereas for a child with a semantic-pragmatic disorder, intervention is more likely to focus on the communicative functions of language, although not in isolation from the linguistic tools required to achieve communicative goals.

At a more specific level, intervention may target phonological, syntactic, semantic or pragmatic aspects of a child's language, or non-linguistic skills which are felt to provide some of the relevant underpinnings for more efficient language learning, such as attention to sound, turn-taking, representational play or matching and sorting. Within each of these aspects even more specific goals will usually be formulated to guide intervention (Fey, 1986; Harris, 1990; Lees and Urwin, 1991).

In reviewing studies evaluating the effectiveness of language intervention, Nye, Foster and Seaman (1987) found that the largest improvements occurred for syntactic characteristics and the smallest for pragmatic characteristics (although the difference was not statistically significant).

When a child has no speech or only very limited speech, a decision has to be taken as to whether the goals of intervention should include the introduction of an alternative or augmentative communication system to serve in place of or supplement the use of spoken language. Alternative or augmentative communication systems include manual sign languages (such as British Sign Language), more limited systems of manual signs (such as Makaton which uses a vocabulary of signs derived from British Sign Language), symbol systems (such as Blissymbolics and the Rebus system), pictorial systems and written language. Resistance to the introduction of alternative or augmentative communication systems sometimes occurs on the grounds that they are stigmatising, do not significantly help to reduce social isolation and may prevent the development of spoken language. There is little evidence to support the last of these points. The input to users of alternative or augmentative communication systems typically consists of signs or symbols presented along with speech (either natural or synthesised). Kiernan (1987) reports that children who receive augmentative communication programmes have frequently been found to develop the ability to vocalise and to produce speech.

Decisions about which particular augmentative communication system to introduce can also be contentious, and are likely to be influenced by the relative weightings given to such factors as ease of learning, flexibility of the system as a communication tool, the number and availability of people able to use the system, and cost. For example, symbol systems tend to be easier to learn than sign systems, perhaps because recall memory is required in order to produce the appropriate sign, whereas the appropriate symbol can be selected using only recognition memory (since the set of alternative symbols is usually laid out in front of the child). On the other hand, symbol systems are typically less flexible and powerful as communication tools (Howlin, 1989; Kiernan, 1987). The choice of an augmentative communication system also needs to take into account the characteristics of the individual child, such as his/her cognitive, perceptual and motor skills.

Intervention techniques

A vast range of intervention techniques are used with children who have language or communication disorders, since most clinicians devise individualised programmes based on the needs of the particular child, combined with their own experience of what has proved successful in the past. Nevertheless, these techniques can be grouped into two broad categories: behavioural approaches and naturalistic approaches.

Behavioural approaches

Behavioural approaches to language intervention are based on the principles of learning theory and hence on the assumption that language can be learned through such processes as imitation, reinforcement, shaping, modelling and prompting. For example, if the goal is to teach a child to use personal pronouns (such as 'he' and 'she') appropriately, exercises might be presented in which the child is shown a picture (e.g. of a girl swimming) and is asked a question (e.g. 'What is the girl doing?'). The question could then be followed by a prompt ('Say "she is swimming"') to encourage the child to imitate the appropriate response. A correct imitation could then be reinforced by praising the child. Modelling is similar to imitation, but the child is not asked to reproduce the therapist's utterance immediately. Instead, the child is asked to listen carefully to the therapist producing utterances containing the linguistic forms which are the target of intervention. Then the child is given a turn at speaking in a context similar to the one in which the therapist has modelled the relevant linguistic forms. For instance, the therapist and child may take turns at describing a set of pictures.

There are a number of studies indicating that behavioural techniques can be effective in improving the production of various linguistic forms in children with a specific language disorder. However, children often experience difficulties in generalising what they have learned to related linguistic constructions. Hegde, Noll and Pecora (1979) taught children to use 'is' in sentences beginning with 'he' and found that although the children successfully generalised their use of 'is' to other sentences beginning with 'he', they failed to generalise to sentences beginning with 'she'. Problems can also arise in generalising to situations which differ from the training situation. Leonard (1981) outlines four of the ways in which situations may differ from the training situation: in terms of the visual stimuli talked about (e.g. real situations versus pictures), in terms of the verbal stimuli used as prompts (e.g. open-ended versus explicit questions), in terms of the setting (e.g. home versus clinic), and in terms of the co-conversationalist (e.g. parent versus therapist). On the basis of several studies investigating generalisation effects, Leonard concludes that use of a trained linguistic form is usually successfully generalised to situations which differ from the training situation in only one or two of these respects, but that problems in generalising tend to arise when situations differ in three or four respects. It is therefore important for behavioural training to be conducted in a variety of contexts.

Naturalistic approaches

Naturalistic approaches to language intervention are based on the assumption that children will learn language best in situations where it is being used to serve genuine communicative purposes and where it is closely integrated with real life activities. This assumption is often accompanied by the assumption that children's language problems can be resolved through incidental learning. Thus, the role of the therapist or teacher is not to improve the use of particular linguistic forms through explicit teaching, but rather to facilitate incidental learning of linguistic forms in meaningful communicative contexts by providing appropriate linguistic input and opportunities for the child to use the targeted linguistic behaviour. One way of making communicative contexts meaningful is to base them around activities and topics which are of interest to the child and which relate to her/his experiences. Therefore, naturalistic intervention programmes need to be tailored to the interests of individual children, as well as to their need for an emphasis on a particular type of linguistic input. Another way of ensuring that interventions occur in meaningful, relevant contexts is to carry them out within real life settings, such as the classroom, playground or home, rather than withdrawing the child to a separate room or to a speech and language therapy clinic. This, in turn, encourages collaboration in the intervention process to occur with significant people in the child's life, such as parents, siblings, peers, class teachers and nursery nurses. (Of course, collaboration with at least some of these people can also be encouraged in a clinic setting, but in a more contrived way.) Advocates of naturalistic approaches include Harris (1988) and Watson (1990).

Since the naturalistic approach involves intervening either in everyday settings or in settings designed to mimic everyday settings, problems of generalising what is learned from the therapeutic situation to real life situations are avoided or substantially reduced. Bochner et al. (1980) present two case-studies which highlight typical differences between the naturalistic approach and the more traditional behavioural approach. One five year old who had a language disorder and a suspected mild mental handicap received language intervention based on the behavioural approach, whereas another five year old who had similar problems received intervention based on the naturalistic approach. Both children made progress in language skills, but the nature of this progress differed between the two children. The child who had received behavioural intervention acquired the skills she had been drilled in, such as labelling pictures and objects and answering direct questions, but she did not succeed in generalising these skills to normal conversations with her teachers and peers when she moved from a special education class into a mainstream class. In contrast, the child who had received the naturalistic intervention did acquire spontaneous language skills which generalised to the new setting of a mainstream class. Bochner et al. see their findings as evidence for the claim that 'children learn what they are taught' (1980). Although this conclusion is based on a qualitative study of only two children, it is broadly consistent with the conclusion reached by Leonard (1981) on the basis of more extensive evidence (from a review of studies). He concludes that training which focuses only on particular linguistic forms tends to yield effects limited to the child's use of these forms, whereas training with a more general focus usually results in broader linguistic gains.

When considering issues of generalisation, it is important to remember that the contexts in which children are likely to have to deploy linguistic skills are not restricted to low-structure, informal contexts in which language is closely linked to their own immediate purposes and concerns. It is true that such contexts predominate in the life of a young child, but if the child is to progress successfully in the educational system, he will also have to cope with more formal contexts in which language is 'disembedded' from immediate purposes (Donaldson, 1978). In particular, the ability to use and understand language in disembedded contexts, and perhaps also to reflect on the formal properties of language, is likely to be crucial to the acquisition of literacy. Such considerations become especially significant in the light of the evidence indicating that children with spoken language disorders are at risk of encountering reading problems (Silva, McGee and Williams, 1983).

The naturalistic approach has considerable intuitive appeal since it is consistent with contemporary theories of normal language acquisition. Although such theories differ in whether they emphasise innate knowledge of the structural properties of language or the acquisition of language within supportive social contexts, they have in common an eschewal of the role of explicit language teaching by adults. However, despite the superficial plausibility of the argument that intervention procedures for children with language disorders should aim to mimic the processes by which language is normally acquired, some caution is called for. It does not necessarily follow that the 'normal' developmental route is the best route for all children. The very fact that children with language disorders have not made normal progress in acquiring language 'naturally' suggests that an alternative approach may be beneficial or even necessary.

Of course, most naturalistic intervention approaches are alternative approaches in the sense that they aim to adapt normal interactions to the child's needs, by for example providing extra opportunities to observe and practise linguistic forms or functions which are posing problems. However, as Conant et al. (1984) point out, a potential difficulty is that opportunities to work on particular problem areas may not arise sufficiently frequently in natural situations. Furthermore, considerable skill and ingenuity on the part of the teacher or therapist is required in order to exploit naturally occurring opportunities for intervention.

Conant et al. devised an intervention programme which aimed to combine the advantages of traditional behavioural approaches with those of incidental learning approaches. Their programme consisted of a set of communication games in which particular features of syntax, vocabulary or articulation could be focused upon, but in which these features served the same pragmatic functions as in normal conversation. In these games, the roles of speaker and hearer were alternated between the child and the teacher. For example, hiding games were used in which the child and the teacher took turns at guessing where an object was hidden. The materials for this game could be constructed in such a way as to encourage the use of particular linguistic forms in the guesses. The feedback which the child received related not to arbitrary standards of 'correctness' but to the communicative adequacy or inadequacy of his messages (e.g. whether the child succeeded in communicating his guess to the adult so that she could look for the object in the place the child had intended). Conant et al. found that children who received their intervention programme over a period of four months made more progress (in terms of the quality of their spontaneous speech) than an untreated control group. This effect applied to children whose language disorder was accompanied either by a moderate cognitive delay or by no cognitive delay. It did not hold for children who had a severe cognitive delay.

These findings illustrate the effectiveness of 'compromise' approaches which combine features from the behavioural and naturalistic approaches to intervention. Similar approaches have been devised by several other authors. Howlin (1989) reports that in recent years behavioural approaches to intervention have become less artificial and that behavioural techniques are now usually employed in communicatively meaningful contexts. She further suggests that the degree of structure which is appropriate in a language intervention approach will depend on characteristics of the child. In particular, she proposes that more highly structured programmes may be best suited to children with very limited linguistic skills or those with limited motivation to communicate (e.g. severely autistic children).

In summary, most of the available intervention techniques have been shown to produce some positive effects, but no particular technique stands out as being more effective overall than other techniques. The literature also suggests that different techniques produce different types of positive effects and that different techniques are probably appropriate for different types of children. However, clear and detailed evidence is lacking on which techniques are best suited to which children. In the circumstances, the best strategy is likely to be to adopt an eclectic and individualised approach to intervention.

Settings of intervention

Children with language disorders are to be found in a wide range of educational settings, such as mainstream nursery schools and schools, various types of special schools, and special classes or units (for example, language units). In addition, preschool children with language disorders may be attending playgroups or nurseries (run privately or by the social work department), or they may not be receiving any form of preschool provision. Language intervention may take place within any of these settings or in a speech and language therapy clinic (either within or outwith one of these settings) or in the home. We will now look in some detail at the nature of the provision within one particular type of setting, namely language units.

Language units are of particular interest in that they aim to cater specifically for children with language disorders and to promote collaboration amongst different types of professional, especially teachers, speech and language therapists and educational psychologists. Also, they represent a compromise between mainstream and special education.

Surveys of language units in Scotland (Working Party of Scottish Principal Educational Psychologists, 1988) and in Britain as a whole (Donlan, 1987) have revealed that language units vary considerably on a number of dimensions.

First, they vary in terms of the age range which they cater for. Some units cater for children of any age within the preschool and primary age range, whereas other units cater for only part of this age range. There are very few language units for secondary school age children in Britain.

Second, different language units have different admission criteria. In the Scottish survey, it was found that approximately half of the teachers (from the twelve units surveyed in detail) were able to give clearly defined admission criteria, whereas the other half said either that there were no rigid criteria or that they themselves were not directly involved in admission procedures. There were three criteria on which there was a clear consensus among staff from different units:

1. a need for intensive speech therapy;
2. mainstream children with specific language difficulties;
3. exclusion of other major primary causes of failure to develop language (mental, physical, emotional or sensory).

However, when staff were asked (in another questionnaire) to describe the characteristics of the children who were actually attending their unit, 75% of the children were described as having other significant difficulties, with 26% of children being described as having 'cognitive difficulties resulting in generalised delay or learning difficulties' and 22% as having 'social/emotional difficulties'. Of course, some of these other difficulties may have been secondary effects rather than primary causes of the children's linguistic difficulties. However, even allowing for this and for the fact that about 50% of units were not able to state rigid admission criteria, it appears that there may sometimes be discrepancies between admission policy and admission practice. Similarly, Donlan (1987) reports that in his survey 32% of units showed a discrepancy between the staff's descriptions of the children's problems and the stated admission criteria. Furthermore, in relation to the specific criterion of normal non-verbal intelligence, Donlan writes:

> Of those stating criteria only 45% included the requirement of non-verbal ability within the average range. Good practice in the longer established Units and Schools continues to emphasise the importance of establishing a deficit in verbal versus non-verbal levels of functioning. But present trends in Educational Psychology appear to be in dispute with this practice . . .

The argument that language unit admission should be restricted to children with specific language disorders is based partly on an underlying assumption that general cognitive development constrains linguistic development and therefore that children whose language problems are associated with a general cognitive delay are less likely to benefit from the interventions provided in language units. However, these assumptions are not entirely clearcut. There has been a historical shift in the theories which psycholinguists have postulated regarding relationships between cognitive and linguistic development. For example, Cromer originally advanced the Cognition Hypothesis which states that linguistic development is constrained by cognitive development, but he has since revised this to a much less extreme and more complex position in which he argues that linguistic abilities can sometimes develop far in advance of non-verbal intelligence (Cromer, 1991). It is true that language problems have been found to resolve less readily for children with IQs below the normal range, but this could be interpreted as an argument either for or against admitting such children to a language unit. Furthermore, when Cole, Dale and Mills (1990) compared a group of children who had cognitive skills markedly above their linguistic skills with a group whose cognitive and linguistic skills were similarly impaired, they found that both groups benefited from language intervention over a one year period. It is also important to recognise that research has so far failed to identify a single underlying cause for specific language impairment (SLI), that children with SLI probably do not themselves constitute a homogeneous group and that many of them do show various subtle non-linguistic difficulties, for example with auditory processing or symbolic play (Reid and Donaldson, 1993).

Another argument which may underlie all three of the admission criteria which were identified in the survey is that since language unit placement is a scarce and expensive resource, it should be targeted on those children for whom enhanced language skills would make unsupported mainstream education a realistic goal.

A third respect in which language units vary is in terms of their relationships to mainstream schools. Of the twelve units studied in detail in the Scottish survey, eight were situated in mainstream primary schools, one in a mainstream nursery school, two in child guidance clinics and one in a hospital. In most of the units attached to schools, opportunities for integration were limited to locational integration (being on the same site) and social integration (mixing socially at break times). A few of the units also had some functional integration in which the children from the language unit shared some educational activities with children from the mainstream part of the school. Only one unit tried to re-introduce children gradually to mainstream schooling before they returned to a mainstream school on a permanent, full-time basis. However, in half of the units catering for primary school age children the children attended the unit only part-time and most of them spent the rest of the school week in a mainstream school.

The nature of staffing also varies from unit to unit. The most usual pattern in the Scottish survey was for the full-time staff to be a teacher and a nursery nurse or auxiliary, with educational psychologists and speech therapists being part-time members of staff. However, one unit had a full-time speech therapist and another unit was run on the basis of part-time input from speech therapists without any input from teachers. Some units had one educational psychologist working in the unit on a regular basis, whereas other units had several psychologists participating as case workers. The latter arrangement was regarded as unsatisfactory both by the psychologists and by the teachers. Since most units were staffed by more than one type of professional, it appears superficially at least that there was an interdisciplinary approach to intervention. However, it was found that the week's activities were decided upon by a multidisciplinary team in only half the units. In the other units, this decision was made by the person in charge (who was usually a teacher).

As part of the survey, language unit staff were asked what they saw as their roles within the unit. The most frequently mentioned role for speech therapists was assessment, for psychologists it was involvement in future placement, for teachers it was group and class teaching, and for nursery nurses it was creating and supervising play experiences. However, each group also mentioned various other roles fairly frequently and there was some overlap between professions in these.

For example, speech therapists, psychologists and teachers were all involved in assessment, reviews and devising individual intervention programmes. It is unclear to what extent this overlap in roles is indicative of collaboration as opposed to duplication of effort or even conflict.

When the staff were asked how they would like their roles to change, it was found that the speech therapists and psychologists were the groups who most wanted changes. The speech therapists frequently expressed a desire to be more involved in working in the classroom, in collaboration with teachers and using a less formal approach to intervention. This is consistent with the increasing shift towards more naturalistic intervention approaches. The psychologists typically wanted to spend more time in the unit working with the staff on communication approaches and they also wanted to work more with parents.

Parental involvement in the units was found to be very limited. The Working Party concluded that:

> In most units consideration was given to the concept of partnership, but little evidence of it occurred in practice. There was no evidence of parents taking an active part in decision-making processes.

In view of the value of parental involvement, this is clearly a matter for concern.

One of the most interesting aspects of the Scottish Working Party's survey concerns the staff's perceptions of the advantages of the language unit. Answers to the question 'What does the unit have to offer to help children's language development?' showed a high degree of consistency across professions. The most frequent responses were 'a high staff ratio enabling individual and small group teaching' (given by 74% of respondents); 'understanding of the children's needs – a supportive environment' (52%); 'a curriculum geared to developing language and communication' (46%); and speech therapy provision (46%). It is interesting to note that responses relating specifically to language came third in this list, which is perhaps surprising in the light of the emphasis given to specific language disorders in the criteria for admission to many language units. The characteristics of the units mentioned in the two most frequent responses are ones which are likely to be beneficial to any special needs child or indeed to any child. A related question asked staff to specify the approaches which they felt were most helpful to children's communication development. Once again, there was a considerable degree of consensus in responses to this question. The most frequent responses referred to games and free play, real life situations and child-centred approaches encouraging spontaneous child-initiated communication. This clearly indicates a commitment to naturalistic approaches to intervention, although no evidence is provided on the extent to which this commitment was put into practice.

An important question is whether language units are effective in remediating children's language disorders, but unfortunately there are very few studies addressing this question. Urwin, Cook and Kelly (1988) followed up children who had attended a preschool language unit and whose ages at follow-up ranged from six to eleven years. They found that 84% of the children were in mainstream schools. These children were judged by their teachers to be well-integrated members of their class and to have made progress over the previous twelve months. Urwin et al. report that the average verbal IQ and general IQ for the group at follow-up were in the low average range (89 and 94, respectively). However, in the absence of data on the children's scores before entry to the language unit and in the absence of a comparison group who had not attended a language unit, it is difficult to see what can be concluded about the effectiveness of language units from these findings.

A similar but more thorough study was conducted by Bruges (1988). She found that 22% of the children who had been discharged from a language unit were still in some form of special education. The children's current teachers were asked to rate their academic achievement and social skills. For academic attainment, 21% of the children were rated as 'average', 38% as 'below average' and 40% as being 'in the bottom 10%'. In terms of social skills, 68% of the children were rated as mixing well with their peers. Bruges argues that these findings suggest a better outcome than would be predicted from the findings of the National Child Development Study (1978) in which 50% of children who had language problems at seven years showed residual language, learning, social and emotional problems at sixteen years. However, the validity of such a comparison is highly questionable since it is unclear how Sheridan and Peckham's category of 'residual problems' maps on to the rating categories used in Bruges' study. Furthermore, as Bruges herself points out, her findings do not permit any conclusions to be drawn about which aspects of language unit provision were responsible for any beneficial effects, nor about which types of children were most likely to benefit.

On the basis of the currently available evidence, the verdict on the efficacy of language units has to be 'not proven'. Indeed, obtaining conclusive evidence on the efficacy of language units is a far from straightforward task. As the survey of Scottish language units showed, there are considerable variations amongst language units in both practice and policy, so it may not be meaningful to ask about the efficacy of language unit provision in general. There are also difficulties in identifying suitable groups of children with whom children in language units could be compared to evaluate the efficacy of language unit provision. One of the common reasons for selecting particular children for placements in a language unit is that their language difficulties are severe and have not responded to speech and language therapy prior to admission to the unit. Therefore, such children are by definition likely to differ from other children with specific language impairments who are in other forms of educational provision (such as mainstream schools). If group studies are to be carried out, it is essential to consider how the groups compare on a range of measures taken before the language unit placement begins, as well as assessing how much change occurs during and after the period of intervention. However, a more fruitful initial approach to addressing questions about the efficacy of language units might be to conduct a series of case-studies in which the progress of individual children would be closely monitored before, during and after placement in particular language units and in which the nature of provision in these language units would be documented in detail.

Conclusions

It is impossible to provide unequivocal answers to such questions as 'Which intervention techniques are most effective for helping children with language and communication difficulties?' or 'How effective are particular intervention settings, e.g. language units?' This is partly because of the dearth of research studies addressing such issues of efficacy. However, even when more evidence does become available, it is likely that the answers will be complex, due to variations amongst different types of language and communication disorders, amongst individual children who have similar types of disorders, and amongst different language units.

The complexity of the picture underlines rather than diminishes the need for a principled approach to intervention, in which thorough assessment procedures are used as a basis for formulating clearly specified goals and for devising individualised programmes of intervention. There is increasing recognition of the value of eclectic intervention techniques which combine features of the behavioural and naturalistic approaches to intervention. An important feature of naturalistic approaches is their emphasis on integrating the interventions with the child's everyday activities and experiences. Such integration is likely to be enhanced in situations where there is a high level of collaboration amongst parents, teachers, nursery nurses, speech and language therapists and educational psychologists. Language units aim to promote cross-disciplinary collaboration and parental involvement, although the extent to which these aims are realised in practice is difficult to establish and almost certainly varies across units. An important question for future research to address is how effective collaboration amongst parents and professionals can best be achieved, not only in language units but also in other settings.

References

Bochner, S., Price, P., Salmon, L., Yeend, G. and Orr, E. (1980) Language intervention: a classroom report. *British Journal of Disorders of Communication*, **15**, 87-102

Bruges, A. (1988) The outcome of language unit placement: a survey in Avon. *Educational Psychology in Practice*, **4**, 86-90

Cole, K.N., Dale, P.S. and Mills, P.E. (1990) Defining language delay in young children by cognitive referencing: are we saying more than we know? *Applied Psycholinguistics*, **11**(3)

Conant, S., Budoff, M., Hecht, B. and Morse, R. (1984) Language intervention: a pragmatic approach. *Journal of Autism & Developmental Disorders*, **14**, 301-317

Cromer, R.F. (1991) *Language and Thought in Normal and Handicapped Children*. Oxford, Blackwell

Crystal, D. (1982) *Profiling Linguistic Disability*. London, Edward Arnold

Dewart, H. and Summers, S. (1988) *The Pragmatics Profile of Early Communication Skills*. Windsor, NFER Nelson

Donaldson, M. (1978) *Children's Minds*. Glasgow, Collins/Fontana

Donaldson, M.L. (1992) *Children with Language and Communication Disorders: a review of the literature*. Report commissioned by the Scottish Office Education Department

Donlan, C. (1987) Adequate provision? The ICAA survey of language units. In *Language Units – a review*, eds. J. Stone and M. Kersner. London, National Hospitals College of Speech Sciences

Fey, M.E. (1986) *Language Intervention with Young Children*. London, Taylor & Francis

Harris, J. (1988) *Language Development in Schools for Children with Severe Learning Difficulties*. London, Croom Helm

Harris, J. (1990) *Early Language Development: Implications for Clinical and Educational Practice*. London, Routledge

Hegde, M., Noll, M. and Pecora, R. (1979) A study of some factors affecting generalization of language training. *Journal of Speech and Hearing Disorders*, **44**, 301-320

Howlin, P. (1989) Changing approaches to communication training with autistic children. *British Journal of Disorders of Communication*, **24**, 151-168.

Kiernan, C. (1987) Non-vocal communication systems: a critical survey. In *Language Development and Disorders,* eds. W. Yule and M. Rutter. Oxford, Blackwell/MacKeith Press

Knowles, W. and Masidlover, M. (1982) *Derbyshire Language Scheme* (Revised ed.). Ripley, Derbyshire Educational Psychology Service

Lees, J. and Urwin, S. (1991) *Children with Language Disorders*. London, Whurr

Leonard, L. B. (1981) Facilitating linguistic skills in children with specific language impairment. *Applied Psycholinguistics*, **2**, 89-118

Nye, C., Foster, S. H. and Seaman, D. (1987) Effectiveness of language intervention with the language/learning disabled. *Journal of Speech and Hearing Disorders*, **52**, 348-357

Reid, J. and Donaldson, M. L. (1993) Specific language impairment: explanations and implications. In *Specific Learning Difficulties (Dyslexia), Perspectives on Practice,* ed. G. Reid. Edinburgh, Moray House Publications

Sheridan, M. D. and Peckham, C. (1978) Follow-up to 16 years of school children who had marked speech defects at 7 years. *Child: Care, Health and Development,* **4**, 145-157

Silva, P.A., McGee, R.O. and Williams, S. M. (1983) Developmental language delay from three to seven years and its significance for low intelligence and reading difficulties at age seven. *Developmental Medicine and Child Neurology*, **29**, 630-640

Urwin, S., Cook, J. and Kelly, K. (1988) Preschool language intervention: a follow-up study. *Child: Care, Health and Development*, **14**, 127-146

Watson, J. (1990) Language facilitation in the classroom. *British Journal of Special Education*, **17**(4), 143-147

Working Party of Scottish Principal Educational Psychologists (1988) *Children with Communication Difficulties*. Available from Dr J. Watson, Moray House Institute of Education, Edinburgh.

Developing the Foundations of Communicative Competence in Children with Severe Physical Disability

Alison MacDonald and Caroline Rendle

Introduction

The field of augmentative and alternative communication (AAC) has been developing for at least the last fifteen years, from tentative beginnings in the 1970s when attention first focused on teaching an alternative linguistic code to replace the spoken medium. Many of the early sign and symbol users have now grown up and we are able to look at how they are making use of their communication systems.

There are some excellent adult non-vocal, augmented communicators and few people would dispute that this field has opened new and rewarding opportunities for many severely disabled children and adults. There are, however, some facts that have become more obvious as time has moved on, for example:

- mastery of a particular code (be it Rebus or Bliss symbols, an alphabet chart or signs from the Makaton Vocabulary stages) does not ensure that the individual user will function as a competent communicator;
- provision of an expensive communication aid will not ensure that it is used in a versatile and truly interactive way.

How then do we try to ensure that young potential augmentative communication system users eventually become competent adult communicators?

There is increasing evidence that points to the importance of starting augmentative communication programmes early before the child has missed out on rich linguistic and interactional experiences. Children without speech easily settle into the role of passive spectator, without the flexibility to adapt communicative style and mode to suit different communication partners. The problem, however, is that it is not always easy to predict a young child's eventual abilities as an oral communicator and, in any case, it is difficult for parents to let go of their hopes that their child will 'speak'.

We were faced with this dilemma in 1991 when we set up a project at Queen Margaret College with four severely cerebral palsied two-year-olds, to look at how individually targeted speech and language therapy might complement early education groups such as that described by Dairon (1991). First we needed to ask:

> What makes an augmentative communication user a competent communicator?

and secondly:

> How can we devise a programme that will provide an equally sound underpinning to the development of communication through both the spoken and alternative routes?

Our starting point was a paper by Janice Light (1989), in which she suggests that AAC users' eventual communicative competence requires four major components:

- ***linguistic competence*** – adequate mastery of the native language (vocabulary and grammar) plus the code (e.g. signs or symbols) required to operate the augmentative communication system;
- ***operational competence*** – mastery of technical skills required to operate the system, i.e. the motor and cognitive skills required to signal a message or to operate specific device features (pointing, signing, visual scanning, operating switches, controlling cursors, editing, etc.);
- ***social competence*** – knowledge and skill in the social rules of communication (e.g. making appropriate eye-contact, sharing the balance of talking and listening) and using communication for a range of different purposes (social chat, making requests, responding to others, contradicting people, etc.);
- ***strategic competence*** – flexibility in order to adapt communicative style to suit the receiver (e.g. signing more slowly to strangers; turning up the volume on the communication aid in a noisy room), or learning how to correct misunderstanding or to extend the conversation (e.g. if a child cannot explain something clearly on his Touch Talker he might have a message that says, 'Please hold up my Bliss chart, I'd like to explain something').

We felt that it should be possible to create a framework for introducing a broad spread of communication skills to very young children by highlighting some of the essential early skills which need to be developed to support these facets of competence. Also, that by widening Light's description of Operational Competence to include the speech apparatus (as tools with which we communicate) a range of signalling tools including vocal, as well as manual, visual and others, can be facilitated as appropriate.

Under Linguistic Competence we have included the development of symbolic understanding as this is going to influence the eventual choice of augmentative system. The stages we identified (see Appendix) are influenced by the work of Cooper, Moodley and Reynell (1978) and DeLoache (1987).

Early skills towards Strategic Competence include learning to move easily from one mode of communication to another as necessary (e.g. from chart to communication aid; or vocalisation supported by pointing to pictures) and that it is sometimes necessary to clarify one's meaning in a way that is clear to the receiver.

Figure 6.1 shows the resulting model – a pyramid of skills towards eventual communicative competence. This model extends Light's definition of communicative competence to provide a specific focus on the young child's communicative development.

Fig. 6.1: Early steps towards communicative competence

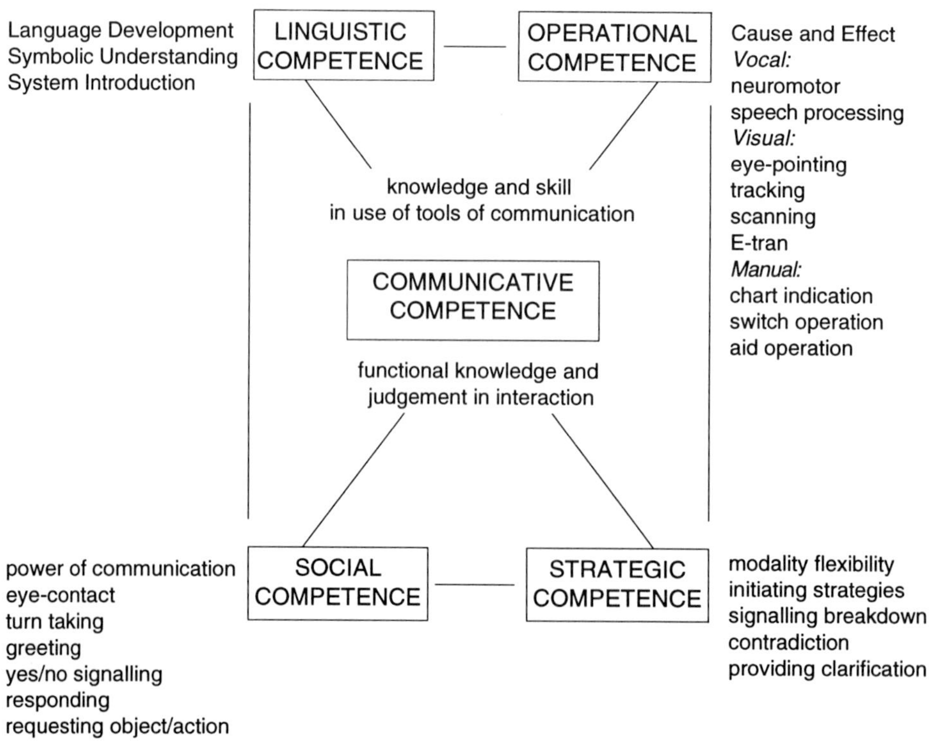

The children

Four children, initially aged between nineteen and thirty-one months were involved in the project. Initial assessment suggested that two of the children, Alan and Carrie, would require long-term augmentative communication support and that the remaining two, Bobby and David, although possibly requiring short-term communication support, showed more potential to eventually develop speech. The children presented as follows.

All four children had reached the early stages of symbolic understanding and intentional use of adults to acquire objects. They all showed understanding of the significance of common everyday objects and some photographs. Early communication skills already exhibited included eye contact, communicative intent, joint attention and emotional signalling of likes and dislikes. They could select a range of real objects on verbal command and a similar range of information was communicated by all, e.g. greetings, accepting/rejecting, object requesting and naming.

Alan had good head control and used eye-gaze purposefully and effectively although he had no sitting balance and limited upper limb function. He was also beginning to develop an understanding of miniature toy representations and at two years was able to reliably select objects by function and to show an understanding of simple positional referents. Alan used his eyes very effectively to communicate single-item ideas but vocal attempts were limited to an open vowel used to gain attention and to signify confirmation. He was also beginning to enjoy joint discussions of past events.

Bobby and David required slight support for sitting and had good control of head and eye movement. Both could reach and were developing manual grasp and release skills. They had a small range of intentional vocalisations which were supplemented by eye-pointing and facial expression. However David, who was only nineteen months on entering the programme, was not yet consistent at selecting from a range of real objects on verbal command.

Carrie was athetoid and had to be optimally positioned to achieve any degree of consistent purposeful movement. When selecting objects on verbal command her responses were unreliable and difficult to confirm due to her poor use of eye-gaze. Carrie used some facial expression and inconsistent eye-pointing to communicate her needs.

Assessment

In order to assess and monitor the development of early communication skills published assessment materials were initially investigated.

Social and pragmatic profiles
Prior to commencing the project, background information was required on each child's communication needs and abilities. Parents were asked to fill in a Communication Environment Form based on the home environment section of Joan Bruno's form (1989). The Pragmatics Profile (Dewart and Summers,1988) was completed by parents and therapist together. This profile, although time-consuming, allows in-depth discussion with the parent on 'what' and 'how' the child is communicating. Also, as several parents commented, it encourages a positive focus on their child's communication.

Linguistic development
For the assessment of linguistic skills, the Reynell Developmental Language Scales (Reynell and Huntley, 1985) were considered. The basic outline of the verbal comprehension section was modified to provide increased opportunities to discover the child's level of linguistic and symbolic understanding. In addition, Tina Bangs' list of language comprehension behaviours (Bangs, 1982) was used to order a section on early concepts of size, position and quantity. This resulted in an assessment with the flexibility to informally test the children over a number of sessions in a play situation.

A section which looked at emerging expressive language skills was also compiled which enabled documentation of intentional communication through various modalities. For this population group there was a need to highlight three aspects: the means of conveying information (e.g. speech, eye-pointing, gesture), the number of items of information conveyed and the communicative functions signalled. The communicative functions were selected with reference to the communicative intention section of the Pragmatics Profile and also to the work of Wirz, Skinner and Dean (1990). This enabled documentation of the frequency of use of modalities and functions, as well as assessment over a period of time in a variety of environments, if necessary.

Symbolic development
Each child's level of symbolic understanding was documented on a checklist based on the stages described in the Appendix.

Operational skills
In order to foster operational competence children with physical disability need to be able to make optimal use of one or more of a range of possible ways in which to communicate their needs. An assessment was needed which looked at visual, oral and upper limb function in order to achieve an overall picture. To communicate through visual means, the child should be able to use eye contact, tracking skills

and scanning, as well as eye-pointing and hand-eye co-ordination. Upper limb control is required for signing, pointing to symbols or accessing technology, so hand function had to be assessed in conjunction with information from occupational therapists. For those children who have the potential to develop speech, assessment of oral control, the frequency of vocalisations, the positions and situations which maximised the use of these vocalisations as well as a description of the type of vocalisations evident was also necessary. From this broad assessment of potential tools it could be seen which modality was primarily being used for communication and also which had potential to be developed.

Using these assessment profiles as a basis the therapy programmes were planned.

Therapy

The therapy sessions always included at least one of the child's parents and were divided into three main strands:

1. symbolic play;
2. computer based activities;
3. active play/Introtalker.

Symbolic play

Doll play is an important vehicle for encouraging decentred symbolic development. Micro-worlds can be created which allow the child with physical disability to experience the language of movement and position that is so often reduced in his personal environment. This can also be incorporated into group work but individual sessions provide opportunities for each child to create his own imaginative, fantasy worlds. It is tempting for doll play to stop at the large doll, realistic object level because cerebral palsied children can be helped to manipulate larger toys and carry out activities themselves in a way that becomes more physically difficult with doll's house miniatures. It seems important, however, to lead them on into increasingly rich symbolic levels in which whole stories can be acted out and in fact all four children were fascinated by small doll play and enjoyed participating both physically and creatively.

The doll play sessions followed the development of symbolic understanding as ordered on the checklist but also had many other underlying aims.

Initially the children were introduced to large doll material and the therapist would guide the child through a simple decentered pretend sequence, e.g. bathtime, mealtime, bedtime. The child would be encouraged to experience the power that increased communicative abilities can offer. The child was encouraged to indicate the chosen object and also to make eye contact with the listener, so that appropriate social skills were also being encouraged. As each child became more secure in the ability to enter this dolls' world, photographs of relevant items were associated with their referents and the children were encouraged to indicate choices through these photographs. The photographic referents also provided facilitation of spoken output for those children for whom this seemed relevant. Later, small doll play was introduced using miniature doll families and dolls' house furniture. In addition to providing opportunities for processing at a more advanced symbolic level these materials gave greater scope for creative play.

These play situations also provided an opportunity for linguistic input where specific vocabulary and early concepts, e.g. object functions or simple positional concepts, could be targeted.

As well as personal choice-making the child was also encouraged to respond to an adult's request, initially retaining one idea and gradually two items. So the child began increasingly to tolerate and give attention to adult direction. Interpretation of adult initiated requests also allowed monitoring of verbal understanding.

Various communication channels were also encouraged, for example vocalisation, word approximation, manual-pointing and eye-pointing. Eye-pointing (E-tran) frames with photographs which could be accessed by eye-gaze were introduced for those eye-pointing children who developed beyond the two item stage. Towards the end of the project, topic pages with a few pictorial Blissymbols were created for one of the children.

Within the doll play routines the child was also encouraged to convey different types of information, e.g. greetings, object requests, accepting/rejecting. The end of the play sequence provided an opportunity for recap and past event discussion, using photographs. The child would relate the information to a third person who had not been so actively involved in the play, e.g. a parent. This also further encouraged social interaction.

Computer based activities

The second strand of the therapy sessions involved simple computer games. Initially the main aim was to develop cause-effect understanding, as well as to continue to develop skills such as attention control and anticipation. The computer also provided an opportunity to encourage the skills required for operational competence.

A BBC computer was available and therefore a range of software suitable for very young children could be considered. The software chosen for use in this project was 'Switch On' from Brilliant Computing and 'Blob 1' (Disc A) from Widgit Software.

Positioning the two-year-olds for computer work was not always easy. In order to give easy access to the switch and a clear, close view of the screen each child was held facing forwards either astride an adult's lap or, in one case, in a small customised seat placed on top of a normal chair. This allowed three of the children to attempt fairly independent manual control. It was not always possible to find an ideal position for Carrie whose control of involuntary movement fluctuated from session to session. However, with adult support, she did manage to effect purposeful switch operation even though her special seat was not available.

Initially a Block switch was used by all the children. This is a small, hinged-flap switch activated by light depression. However, operating this switch was effortful for two of the children so a Wolfson touch switch was introduced. This lies flush with the work surface and is activated by touch alone, allowing the child to experience greater success and to focus more consistently on the cognitive and linguistic aspects of the activities. As the other two children were gradually becoming more vocal a voice-operated switch was introduced. Both children enjoyed vocalising to produce the computer graphics although with one of the children very careful supervision was required to ensure that purposeful vocalisation remained relaxed. It would be very easy to exacerbate an extensor jaw pattern if used indiscriminately. Bobby, who was by then beginning to attempt some two-word utterances (although with a very restricted phonological system), responded particularly well, attempting not just random vocalisations to trigger the switch but increasingly clear yet relaxed word approximations.

As with the symbolic play activity, the computer provided an opportunity to achieve other underlying aims. In a simple picture-building programme photographs were taken of the screen graphics and soon incorporated into the session, the aim being to foster choice-making through the use of clear pictorial symbolic referents. These allowed the children to make choices and to signal requests in a context slightly removed from the actual equipment and activity. The children soon developed favourites amongst the picture-building sets available. A further aim was therefore built into the weekly routine. This involved the child in sharing his interest and creating an image on behalf of another person. He was allowed to choose a picture for himself and was then asked to select one for another person (mother or therapist), having to look at her, listen to what she wanted and then select it from the array of photographs. Throughout this programme there was opportunity for linguistic development through discussion of each of the pictures as it was built up on the screen. Several software programmes were used to encourage anticipation, visual attention and tracking skills. In one activity, in order to develop anticipation and visual-perceptual skills, the child had to decide from a choice of three photographs which animal was partially hidden behind a wall on the screen. When the voice-operated switch was attached to this game the child was encouraged to practise greetings by vocalising or saying 'hello/bye' to each animal as it appeared/disappeared. For the children who continued to use the touch switch the higher levels of this game also introduced early cursor skills.

All four children enjoyed the computer games so that very quickly the visual stimulus of the computer at one side of the room became a trigger for spontaneous child-initiated requests, usually by eye-pointing, gesture or vocalisation, confirmed by indication from a small (2-4 item) photograph display.

Active play/Introtalker

After two fairly sedentary activities it was felt that each child should have an opportunity for active play. This was achieved through activities such as ball games, hide-and-seek and searching games. The aim of each of these activities was once again to develop a range of skills which would underpin eventual competency across the four areas. In one such activity the child would kick a ball into a bin, the lids would be placed on top and the bins moved around. The child would then have to choose which bin to look into before 'walking' to the bin and taking off the lid. The therapist would ask 'is the ball there?' and the child would be expected to indicate 'Yes/No' before having another turn. This activity also encouraged increased attention span, anticipation and social interaction.

Another example would be a simple game of football. Each person would vocalise, call 'me' or give a non-verbal signal when he wanted a turn. This was designed to develop the child's understanding of the power of communication, of control through vocalisation, of cause and effect, and to encourage social interaction, anticipation and turn-taking.

The need for active play diminished over the year, as each child's concentration span for symbolic play and computer activities lengthened. For two of the children this was eventually replaced by informal introduction to a communication aid, an Introtalker (a portable, speech output communication device, using digitised speech). An eight-key overlay was used (although not all of the keys were programmed) and the icons/symbols were photographs.

The Introtalker was introduced in order to give Alan and Carrie early experience of communication through a speech output device. However, it also provided another means of continuing to develop underlying skills such as cause and effect, manual control and visual attention.

The Introtalker was programmed with the names of family members so that the child could use the communication aid to 'call' his parent. It also enabled carefully structured discussions about past/future events concerning the family. Alan showed great enjoyment of this early experience of participating vocally in social interaction. The Introtalker was also programmed to request objects, e.g. ball/car. The child had to 'call' for his choice by accessing the relevant key using his hand/fist, thus also encouraging hand-eye co-ordination. For both children accessing was difficult and the adult had to carefully manipulate the Introtalker to promote success. The child was then rewarded by rolling the car/ball down a slope. The Introtalker was a useful tool for developing some relevant early skills but at this stage it was not felt to be the full answer to the long-term needs of these two children requiring augmentative communication.

Thus within each thirty-minute session the children would usually participate in three activities, each aiming to develop a broad base of skills which would ultimately contribute to communicative competence.

Although each of the three strands of therapy was pre-planned, it was recognised that the children must have the opportunity to initiate and direct activities. The therapist would, therefore, respond to a child's spontaneously initiated request for specific activities if it was appropriate to change the current activity immediately. If not, the child's request would be acknowledged and an agreement reached as to when to move on so that the child was introduced to the concept of negotiation. As well as the opportunity for the child to initiate requests for familiar and well-liked activities, there were also frequent opportunities to make choices within an activity.

To evaluate the effect of this therapy programme, video recordings were taken of each session and while one therapist interacted with the parent and child, the other therapist kept written records using observation sheets divided into four sections:

1. a brief description of the task;
2. the skills or aims that particular task encouraged;
3. comments on the child's responses;
4. suggestions for future sessions.

It was also decided, with the parents' consent, to record their queries and concerns on a parent-therapist discussion sheet. This noted the topics discussed, which speaker had raised the topic and gave a brief description of the discussion. The aim was to see if a pattern of concerns common to all the parents of these very young children with physical disability became apparent.

Individual progress

At the end of the project the children were aged between twenty-five and forty months, having been involved for periods of between six months and nine months. Although no formal control group measures were possible, it is worth commenting on the children's skills in each of the four competences at the end of therapy.

Alan continued to require trunk support in order to achieve good voluntary head control. He needed assistance to grasp and release but could independently operate a block or touch switch and was beginning to cope with two-switch programmes. Alan progressed to an understanding of simple cursor scanning (a star hovers over each of three hidden animals in turn, the animal appearing if the switch is hit at the appropriate time). He could, with effort, reach out to fist point to symbols and continued to use his eyes to communicate effectively by scanning and selecting from an E-tran frame of eight photographs/symbols. Hand-eye co-ordination remained difficult but he responded well to verbal prompting. Alan had a very limited range of vowel sounds, oral movements and phonation were poorly co-ordinated and purposeful vocalisations had a slightly tense quality. He now, however, recognised and used communicatively approximately twenty pictographic Blissymbols and could match these to small toy representations. Linguistically, Alan understood commands containing two items of information and had concepts of size, position and colour. He used a variety of modalities to communicate, primarily eye-pointing but supported by facial expression and increased frequency of vocalisations. Alan also developed early signs of strategic competence: he responded to verbal prompting to repeat or use an alternative modality and understood the need to persevere in order to convey his message.

Bobby had good head control and was beginning to isolate his right index finger for pointing and could operate a computer using a block switch or voice-operated switch. Voluntary control of hand movements was improving and he showed increasing co-ordination of oral movements and phonation. The syllable length of vocalisations was increasing as were the number of word approximations. Bobby developed an understanding of small toy representations and enjoyed imaginative sequences. Linguistically, his verbal comprehension progressed to an understanding of the function of objects and of two elements in a command. He preferred to communicate vocally. He had to be positively encouraged to support his early word approximations (which were rarely functional except in very limited and obvious contexts) with eye-pointing and did not spontaneously use gesture, nor persist in trying to convey his message. However, the type of information which he conveyed expanded to include naming and simple discussion of past/future events.

Carrie's severe physical disabilities and inconsistent performance were evident throughout. However, when Carrie was optimally positioned and motivated she had sufficient head control to visually track round a computer screen, could scan two items and focus briefly on her choice, and could operate the computer using either small finger or 'arm-swatting' movements to access a touch switch. She showed enjoyment of small toy material and short imaginative sequences, and she could select, by eye-pointing briefly, from a choice of two objects and occasionally from up to four photographs. She also began to use a left arm swat to indicate 'yes' and this was becoming increasingly consistent.

David had good head control, could grasp and release objects with assistance and was beginning to use his left index finger for pointing. His co-ordination of oral movements and phonation was poor. Spontaneous vocalisation was frequent and fairly effortless but purposeful vocalisations, although increasing in frequency, led to increased laryngeal tension. David's symbolic development progressed from an understanding of real objects to photographs, coloured pictures and small toy material. His willingness to respond to adult suggestions developed and he showed verbal understanding of object labels, the function of objects and the ability to retain two key ideas. David understood the need to use a variety of modes of communication. He supported his vocalisations by eye-pointing, fist-pointing and occasionally by using gross gestures. He had definite ideas and would persist until his message had been interpreted. The type of information he conveyed expanded to include requesting and simple discussion of past/future events.

Individual therapy sessions appeared to provide a suitable setting for the introduction of new symbolic referents. All the children became less egocentric and progressed through at least two stages of early symbolic development. One child, Alan, progressed beyond the pictorial line drawings stage and for him, after much discussion, Blissymbols were eventually chosen, symbols being introduced in appropriate play settings. While more visually and cognitively complex symbols (e.g., television) were initially introduced in embellished form (pictorial additions in a paler colour) it was soon clear that, provided the child's full attention was held and explanations were carefully tailored to his interests and life experience, he showed no difficulty in retaining these symbols in their standard form.

Justification for individual speech therapy

There are many excellent and well-founded arguments for the value of group work. We would argue, however, that additional individual sessions provide certain essential requirements for these more cognitively able pre-nursery-school children whether their potential lies in the direction of speech or non-vocal communication.

The majority of communication exchanges are personal one-to-one shared events involving appropriate eye contact, a range of signalling modes and listener-speaker turn-taking. Individual child and parent sessions allow the therapist to demonstrate appropriate interactive behaviour and learning activities which are specifically tailored to each child. They also provide important opportunities for parents to demonstrate and discuss their child's most newly acquired skills.

Materials can be chosen to match each individual child's needs and interests. Some young cerebral palsied children, for example, are sensitive to certain textures such as the fuzzy hair of a doll or the tickly fluff of a soft toy. Others particularly enjoy close assisted manipulation of cuddly toys.

Individual sessions provide a non-distracting framework for the development of concentration and sustained attention to a progressive activity. Group sessions, while fulfilling other needs, may easily create distractions and while fostering turn-taking within a wider framework it is not uncommon to see young children switching off for large portions of time from the main group activity. The attention control of all the children in the project progressed both in their ability to maintain their focus of attention and also in their ability to tolerate adult direction. While it is not possible to say how much of this was due to natural maturation it was very clear that two of the children in particular were retaining new learning extremely well (see following discussion on computer based activities).

Activities leading towards operational competence also require individual assessment and planning. Programmes to encourage early vocal communication need to be based on careful analysis of each child's neuro-motor abilities in addition to evidence of any emerging phonological system. Switch operation is usually enhanced not only by careful positioning of the child but also as a result of trial and error practice. For each child to build up his skills in manual switch control he therefore needs a stretch of successive attempts over which to improve his performance. This can only be carried out in an individual setting where other children are not kept waiting for turns. All children were encouraged to use eye-gaze as a supplementary means of communication. For three of the children eye-transfer (E-tran) frames were introduced. This method of symbol accessing requires a direct face-to-face position between signaller and recipient and while it can eventually be used with a partner in a larger group situation, the introductory stages require carefully directed person-to-person interaction.

Computer based activities

A particularly successful aspect of the intervention programme with these fairly cognitively able but severely physically disabled children has been the inclusion of simple computer programmes. It seems appropriate, therefore, to give some further discussion to this.

In the minds of many professionals the use of computers is still strongly linked to an educational setting; to their use as classroom tools whether to facilitate expressive output or for their educational and training value. The use of more dedicated microtechnology in the form of communication aids has, in recent years, extended downwards into the preschool years, for example some of the introductory Introtalker programmes. There are also several excellent graphics-based computer programmes which, used selectively within the sessions, seemed to facilitate a large number of relevant skills.

Initially the inclusion of single-switch computer programmes was with a view to developing an understanding of cause and effect. When, in the early 1980s, computer software began to become available for physically disabled children it was common to find that the more cognitively impaired child had great difficulty in understanding the link between himself, the switch/keyboard and the screen. Increasingly, therefore, switch-operated toys have been used to encourage this rather specific aspect of three-way interaction.

All the children made rapid progress in understanding the cause and effect link between switch and screen graphics. Concentration was excellent, the cumulative picture-building programmes in particular encouraging sustained attention so that after a few sessions, familiarity with the material could be used as a basis for work on language learning, anticipation, Yes/No responses and repair (e.g. 'what do we need next?'; 'does he have shoes on his head?').

The computer graphics with accompanying intrinsic rewards (a new part of the picture appears in response to each hit) and final rewards (music or a visual activity on the screen) are clearly highly motivating to young children. It was not surprising, therefore, to find such well sustained concentration from all the children, even the nineteen month old. This fits in well with Cooper, Moodley and Reynell's second stage of attention control in which children, normally in the second year of life, will concentrate well on a task of their own choice (Cooper et al., 1978). By Stage 3 children can be more easily deflected from the task underway to an adult's verbal comment and discussion and back again, in other words their focus is becoming more flexible. It was pleasing therefore to see that all these children as they matured into their third year of life were able increasingly to accept adult directed choices and wishes in addition to their own. This was seen as an important aspect of early social and strategic development which is so often poorly developed in children with severe motor impairment. Their wishes are often either too readily attended to by over-solicitous adults or completely unregistered leading to frustration and sometimes eventually to apathy. It seems important therefore to foster a sense of sharing that goes beyond the more basic turn-taking and shared-focus routines which provide such an essential underpinning to all social interaction. In this instance the children not only learned to select according to other people's wishes but also to carry this further into the sustained action of creating a picture 'for Mummy', etc.

The evidence from this project, involving a very small group of four children, seems to be that there is considerable value in introducing simple switch-operated computer activities to pre-nursery-school children. There are, of course, some disadvantages. We found, for example, that parents were on the whole excited and pleased at this somewhat glamorous evidence of their child's abilities. The computer, however, was being used not as an end in itself but in order to foster a range of skills which will hopefully provide a good base for the future work of our colleagues in the nurseries and schools to which the children proceed. As the children progress and mature these colleagues will make decisions on the most appropriate direction for each child. It was important therefore to ensure that parents did not over interpret its value and rush out to buy a rather non-portable computer that is rapidly being superseded. The sessions were set up essentially to work with both children and their parents with a view to demonstrating ideas that could be incorporated into the child's home routine. The computer work could not, of course, be easily followed up in this way. A very encouraging finding, therefore, was that there was real evidence of learning from one week to the next. There were occasional off-days associated with mood or health but all the children learned and built upon their once weekly experiences in a way that was convincing and rewarding. With cognitively able cerebral palsied children there seems to be ample justification for introducing computer work at this very early stage with a view to facilitating not just manual control and an understanding of cause and effect but a range of cognitive, visual, social and linguistic skills.

Parent-therapist discussions

As previously mentioned, parent-therapist discussions were recorded over the nine month period. Some common parental concerns became evident and the type of information discussed also revealed common themes.

Typical topics raised by parents of these two to three year olds concerned therapeutic aims, future therapy provision, schooling and the inter-relating of those concerns. Parents clearly felt a need to raise these discussions and that the individual therapy situation was an appropriate time.

The therapist also gained a valuable and more holistic view of the child through the parent's willingness to describe family situations, the involvement of other carers, the child's behaviour, preferences and general progress, as well as to report relevant comments from other professionals, e.g. advice on handling from the physiotherapist.

As might be expected, explanations concerning the aims of the activities and advice on how to carry over these activities into the home environment were repeated on several occasions by the therapist in order to ensure that they were fully understood. Parents were also provided with opportunities to report back on the success of these suggestions, and they would often include descriptions of their child's vocalisations showing that this was still seen as an area upon which they continued to focus considerable attention.

The amount of discussion generated by the parents concerning future educational placement increased as their child approached nursery school age (three years). These discussions were concerned not only with the search for suitable education but also with the various philosophies associated with the management of children with a physical disability.

This collating of incidental discussion that arose both during and after the therapy sessions confirms the need for therapists to have good listening skills and an awareness of early counselling techniques, to know when to refer to or liaise with other team members and when it is appropriate to give advice. It also seemed to support parents' need to have opportunities to discuss their child on a one-to-one basis with an involved professional even if the discussions were frequently repetitive and covered recurring topics.

Conclusion

Communication is a flexible, multi-faceted ability that takes place in an enormous variety of settings. Children, therefore, need to develop their own communicative skills to meet these varied situations. By keeping in mind the pyramid of underlying skills (Figure 6.1) it should be possible to offer the severely physically disabled child a truly integrated programme from the point at which he is beginning to show cognitive readiness for a move into true linguistic communication. In this way increased opportunities for balanced, holistic development across all four dimensions of communicative competence can be ensured.

References

Bangs, T. (1982) *Language and Learning Disorders of the Pre-academic Child: A Curriculum Guide*. Prentice Hall

Bruno, J. (1989) Customizing minspeak system for a preliterate child: a case example. *Augmentative and Alternative Communication,* **5 (2)**

Cooper, J., Moodley, M. and Reynell, J. (1978) *Helping Language Development. A Developmental Programme for Children with Early Language Handicaps*. Edward Arnold Ltd

Dairon, C. (1991) Early education for under three year olds with multiple impairments. In *Innovatory Practice and Severe Learning Difficulties,* ed. J. Watson. Edinburgh, Moray House Publications

DeLoache, J. S. (1987) Rapid change in the symbolic functioning of very young children. *Science,* **238**, 1556-1557

Dewart, H. and Summers, S. (1988) *The Pragmatics Profile of Early Communication Skills*. Windsor, NFER Nelson

Light, J. (1989) Towards a definition of communicative competence in individuals using augmentative and alternative communication systems. *Augmentative and Alternative Communication,* **5 (2)**

MacDonald, A. and Rendle, C. (1992) 'An Investigation into the Requirements of the Speech Therapy Complement to Early Education Groups for Cerebral Palsied Children'. Unpublished research report

MacDonald, A. and Rendle, C. (1993) Laying the foundations of communicative competence for very young children. In *Augmentative Communication in Practice: Scotland,* eds. H. Galloway and S. Millar. Edinburgh, CALL Centre

Reynell, J. K. and Huntley, M. (1985) *Reynell Developmental Language Scales* (2nd Revision). Windsor, NFER Nelson

Wirz, S., Skinner, C. and Dean, E. (1990) *Revised Edinburgh Functional Communication Profile*. Tucson, Arizona, Communication Skill Builders Inc.

Appendix: Symbolic Development

This refers to the child's increasing ability to understand that representations of decreasing perceptual similarity to the original object may act as a symbolic reference.

Real objects and large dolls
The infant begins to extend his focus beyond himself, to recognise the significance of commonly used objects and to play with these in pretend sequences.

Photographs
Clear coloured photographs are recognised as exact representations of the real item.

Miniatures/small doll materials
These will differ significantly in size and possibly in other visual features from the real item.

Coloured pictures
Two-dimensional but still fairly realistic.

Line drawings (realistic/sketches)
Visually less realistic but still very picture-like.

Line drawings (minimal and stylised)
Simplified outlines as, for example, in pictorial Bliss symbols.

Implementing Language Use 5-14

Margaret Mason

Introduction

This paper is based on a thesis submitted to Newcastle University as partial fulfilment of the requirements for the degree Master of Education for the course 'Child Language and Language Disability'. The study was undertaken in order to investigate the relevance to language disordered children of the new curriculum initiatives for English language in the 5-14 Development Programme and was carried out from January to May 1992 when mainstream class teachers were beginning to incorporate the guidelines into their working practice.

The English language 5-14 guidelines provide a framework composed of four aspects or attainment outcomes of English language: Listening/Watching, Talking, Reading and Writing. Each outcome is divided into a number of strands or aspects of learning. Most strands can be assessed at five levels: A, B ,C, D and E, by means of attainment targets which are specific statements of what a pupil should know or be able to do during primary and secondary education. This study was confined to Level A attainment targets which 'should be attainable in the course of Primary 1 to Primary 3 by almost all pupils'. It is recognised in the language document that progress may not be consistent across the four outcomes of language and that the level of attainment for some pupils may not go beyond or even reach Level A.

It is the school's responsibility to fit the child's needs to the curriculum and attainment targets by implementing the guidelines of English language 5-14 in a way which will result in the provision of 'a language programme which will create the best conditions for personal and social development'. It would appear then, that underneath the English language framework is another agenda which is to do with how the child achieves these attainment targets. For language disordered children this will mean teasing out what the document means and linking it to more specific developmental features. In this way it can act as a diagnostic tool which leads to better planning of an appropriate curriculum. Teaching can then be explicit and clear in specific areas depending on the child's needs .

Section 4 of the English language 5-14 guidelines gives general information on meeting the needs of individual pupils. As there was no specific reference to the implementation of the guidelines with language disordered children the purpose of this study was to:

1. establish if the outcomes of Listening, Talking, Reading and Writing were attainable at Level A by children with a range of language disorders;
2. break down the strands of Listening, Talking, Reading and Writing into smaller steps and evaluate whether or not these could show a child's progression within Level A while taking account of different types of language disorder;
3. evaluate whether or not the attainment results at Level A obtained by the language disordered children demonstrate that the curriculum of the language disordered child requires a greater weighting towards listening and talking than the curriculum of a comparison group of children with no speech and language difficulties;
4. ascertain if English Language 5-14 with the additional steps can be used as a framework for the speech and language therapist, language support teacher and the mainstream class teacher to work together to provide an appropriate curriculum for the language disordered child.

The study was carried out in the Borders Region where provision for language disordered children is provided by the language support service which consists of one full-time and one part-time teacher and a speech and language therapist with 0.7 commitment to the service. This service aims to meet the needs of language disordered children by offering part-time placement in the language base for children with the most severe problems as well as support in mainstream education, advice to teachers and an assessment role.

In order to appreciate the complexity of applying curriculum guidelines to the language impaired population it is necessary to appreciate the diverse nature of this disorder. For the purpose of this study the term 'language disorder' has been used to describe children whose primary difficulty is in the area of speech and/or language, resulting in language which may be quantitatively and/or qualitatively different from normal language learners. A necessary distinction is also made between 'disordered' and 'delayed' language as children with delayed language development may only require low level intervention, an important consideration when allocating resources. The author recognises that language disordered children are not an homogeneous population and that there is no agreed classification. Whilst acknowledging the limitations of any theoretical model of classification of language disorder and the possibility of stereotyped expectations which may result from labelling, a combined medical and linguistic approach was adopted. The three clinical sub-types referred to in this study are:

1. receptive and expressive dysphasia – a difficulty with decoding spoken language which consequently affects encoding;
2. verbal dyspraxia – an impairment in the selection, planning and programming of linguistic and motor schemata for production of language;
3. semantic-pragmatic difficulties – a problem with the content and use of language with relatively little difficulty with language form.

The research

The research took the form of six case-studies of language disordered children. These were the children who received the greatest amount of joint support from the language support teacher and the speech and language therapist in the language base. This group consisted of a Primary 1 child, Alan, with semantic and pragmatic difficulties; two Primary 2 children with verbal dyspraxia, Beth and Colin; two Primary 3 children with verbal dyspraxia, Donald and Euan; and one Primary 5 child, Fergus, with receptive and expressive dysphasia.

A second group of six children were selected to allow for comparison of results between language disordered children and those in mainstream. Two children, considered to be of average ability by their class teachers, from Primary 1, 2 and 3 were chosen so that they could be matched in the first instance by numbers of years in education with the case-study subjects and, with the exception of the Primary 1 children, had reading and spelling ages which corresponded with their chronological age. These children are identified as C1 (male), C2 (female), C3 (male), C4 (female), C5 (male) and C6 (female).

Interviews

At the beginning of the research the six mainstream class teachers of the six language disordered children were interviewed and were asked to estimate the performance of their language disordered child on the 5-14 attainment targets at Level A in Listening, Talking, Reading and Writing. The speech and language therapist and the researcher also estimated the expected performance for the language disordered group on all the attainment targets at Level A. The estimates of performance were recorded according to the system used in the National Reading and Writing Tests which credits a child with:

- A for working at Level A;
- WTA for working towards Level A;
- NRA for not yet ready for Level A.

Assessment tasks

The guidelines expect teachers to devise assessments which reflect the diversity of their work programmes and envisage that attainment targets will be used as a framework for planning assessment. In an attempt to develop assessment tasks and criteria of attainment for each attainment target, a thematic approach was adopted which reflected the everyday working practice in the language base. The theme 'The Farm' was chosen around which the assessment tasks were devised. A farm visit for the twelve children was the starting point. Some of the listening, talking and writing assessments were based on this experience as well as activities which included symbolic play, model making, drawing and painting. Some of the assessment tasks covered more than one outcome.

As the purpose of the study was not only to find out if the language disordered group could achieve Level A attainment targets but also to show the differences in achievement between language and non-language disordered children, additional developmental steps were devised for each attainment target. These aimed to give information on the child's language development. An assessment protocol for all the attainment targets was compiled. The format for each attainment target was as follows:

1. the strand was defined as in English Language 5-14;
2. the attainment target was defined as in English Language 5-14;
3. the assessment task was stated;
4. the criteria for achieving Level A were stated;
5. the developmental steps were stated.

Figure 7.1 shows an example of the format.

The assessment protocol was discussed with mainstream teachers, a speech and language therapist and a teacher who had worked for two years in an advisory role dealing with the introduction of English Language 5-14.

Administration and marking of the assessment tasks

The assessment tasks were administered either individually or in a small group and the pupils' responses were either handwritten by the researcher, audio or video recorded. The researcher analysed all pupil subjects' responses according to the criteria set for obtaining Level A and credited them either A, WTA or NRA. The developmental steps within each level were also credited if obtained. To check the reliability of the researcher's analysis of the results credited to the pupil subjects, the speech and language therapist scored the Listening and Talking assessments from observation of some of the activities, and from the researcher's transcripts of audio-tapes and video recordings. The part-time language support teacher scored the Reading and Writing assessments. Any discrepancies were discussed and a decision of attainment was jointly reached.

Speech and language assessments

The case-study children's speech and language assessment files were examined and any assessments which fell within a re-test date were carried out.

Fig. 7.1

STRAND Talking about experiences, feelings and opinions.

LEVEL A Talk readily about their own experiences and feelings.

TASK A Talk about the visit to the farm.

TASK B Talk about what they enjoyed about the visit and any other feelings about the visit.

CRITERIA FOR ATTAINMENT AT LEVEL A:

Talks readily about the farm visit giving more than two items of information without prompts.

Gives an opinion about the visit.

STEPS

1. Talks with prompts by the teacher. Gives one clause element responses to questions.
2. Produces phrases/sentences with two clause elements, e.g. cow/ born.
3. Produces sentences with three clause elements, e.g. Mummy/licking/baby.
4. Produces sentences with four clause elements, e.g. the shepherd/tied/a plastic coat/around the lamb.
5. Uses correct verb tense to relate experience.
6. Uses co-ordinating conjunctions and, or, but, to form complex sentences.
7. Uses subordinating conjunctions: when, then, first, because.
8. Sequences more than two linked sentences about the experience without prompts.

Results

The following are the results of achievements at Level A for the language disordered group with reference to the performance of the mainstream pupils. It must be emphasised that the results of the Level A assessments are a reflection of a child's performance on that particular day. As language disordered children display fluctuating levels of concentration and motivation it is particularly important to observe and monitor a child over a period of time.

The profiles of attainment of the Level A assessments for the language disordered and the comparison children can be seen in the appendix to this chapter.

Alan

Alan's assessment results on the researcher's protocol and on the standardised language tests are consistent with semantic-pragmatic difficulties in that he had difficulty with the content and use of language and very little difficulty with language form.

At the Primary 1 stage of his education these difficulties showed up in the 5-14 Listening and Talking attainment targets but were not yet evident in the Reading and Writing attainment targets, in which Alan had mastered some of the technical skills required for writing and had developed a sight vocabulary and phoneme/grapheme awareness.

The results of the developmental steps showed that Alan had difficulty engaging with other children in a meaningful and interactive way, as well as difficulty with topic maintenance and the production of appropriate responses to questions.

More specific steps of achievement may need to be added to the protocol in order to monitor progress for this type of child who has difficulty with the meaning of language and its use. These results illustrated the difficulty Alan had sequencing and recalling events in the Talking and Writing strands. This will necessitate a greater weighting of Alan's curriculum towards listening and talking than that of other Primary 1 children.

Beth

The results of the Level A assessment clearly indicated that Beth has language difficulties which span the four language outcomes. Whilst Beth achieved two attainment targets in Listening, C3 and C4 achieved fourteen and fifteen respectively across the four language outcomes. Although Beth's receptive language score on the Test for Auditory Comprehension of Language-Revised (TACL-R) falls just within normal limits the deficit in understanding of vocabulary and concepts on standardised language assessments was not immediately obvious from the Listening steps.

The Talking steps revealed the difference in quantity and quality of Beth's responses and the comparison children. Whilst she was able to give a simple instruction: 'Get bull put in field', C3's instruction was more complex: 'Put the trailer on the tractor and take the bales to the yard'. The steps also showed that Beth gave minimal information such as: 'lambie drinking', 'big and fat', 'walking wobbly', in contrast to a typical response from C3: 'I saw a man putting a sort of plastic coat on the lamb'.

These minimal responses highlight the difficulty Beth has in producing individual words (she scored at the three year level on the Edinburgh Articulation Test), as well as combining words in sentences. As the attainment target for the strand *Audience awareness* requires that the child should talk clearly and audibly to peers and class teacher there is no way of monitoring the development of Beth's speech sound system at her level of difficulty. This suggests that there should be an additional section in English Language 5-14 for language disordered children which monitors phonological development.

The findings clearly indicate that Beth's difficulties with listening and talking are reflected in late development of reading and writing skills. The very specific difficulties Beth has in spoken language are reflected in the minimal amount of information she gives to describe her pictures and an inability to segment sounds in words for spelling which is consistent with her phonological difficulties.

Colin

The standardised language assessment results indicated that Colin's language disorder is mainly confined to aspects of expressive language due to phonological difficulties and poor auditory memory. When Colin's profile of attainments is compared with C3 and C4 he clearly has some difficulty with spoken language but his reading and writing difficulties were more pronounced.

Colin's performance results on the developmental steps in the assessment protocol showed some of the differences in his spoken language compared to the comparison children. Whilst the majority of Colin's utterances were semantically and syntactically correct information was often conveyed in simple sentences demonstrating a difficulty organising more complex constructions. This difficulty was also apparent in a low information score obtained on 'The Bus Story' assessment which assesses continuous speech and requires skill in organising language and memory recall.

The significant feature of these results is the link between Colin's phonological difficulties and his difficulties with organising thought and language to recall events and experiences. Reading and writing development were subsequently delayed.

Donald

The assessment profile for Donald shows that his main difficulties with the Level A attainment targets are in the areas of reading and writing when compared with the comparison children C5 and C6.

The results of Donald's performance on the Level A assessments showed that whilst he was able to use spoken language for a variety of functions, a difficulty with the clarity and fluency of speech remained. These difficulties are clearly attributed to articulation and phonological difficulties which were assessed on the EAT as being at the 3.09 - 4.00 year level. The steps in the assessment protocol did not allow for specific phonological difficulties to be recorded. There was no way of comparing his speech/sound system with the segmentation skills required for reading. The organisational and motor planning difficulties which were apparent in Donald's spoken language were also apparent in his written work.

On 'The Bus Story' assessment Donald's score for average sentence length was above, and his information score below, his chronological age. This indicated that Donald had lots to say but did not always organise his thoughts sequentially or distinguish the relevant information. These difficulties did not however prevent him from reaching Level A in Listening and Talking.

Euan

Euan, who was identified as having phonological difficulties preschool, was by Primary 3 able to achieve most of the Listening and Talking attainment targets but his reading and writing development were behind his comparison pupils.

Whilst Euan was able to express himself clearly in a one-to-one situation he talked quietly in the group situation revealing a lack of confidence and showing an unwillingness to be involved. An analysis of the developmental steps indicated that whilst Euan did not have difficulty with the language structures he used, these were less complex than the comparison children. This matches with his average sentence length on continuous speech being at the four year level on 'The Bus Story' assessment. So although Euan was able to achieve some of the Listening and Talking attainment targets it would appear that he still needed an immense amount of help in those aspects of language for the development of reading and writing skills which were shown to be either at the NRA or WTA stage on assessment.

Fergus

Fergus's performance on receptive language tests showed a big deficit especially with the understanding of grammatical morphemes and elaborated sentences. His expressive language scores were also very low for his age. Despite these low scores he achieved all Level A assessments in Listening, Talking and Writing. Fergus at the time of assessment was ten years one month. His profile of attainment shows that he had difficulty at Level A in reading. Whilst Fergus had learnt to read and was able to decode written language sufficiently for some of the Level A assessments the study found that he still had difficulty making sense of what he read and he did not choose to read for enjoyment.

Discussion

The verbal dyspraxic group

Although Beth, Colin, Donald and Euan share the same classification of language disorder, that of verbal dyspraxia, they attained a range of achievements on the listening and talking steps due to differences in age, level of intelligence, life experiences and severity of disorder. Analysis of the developmental steps showed that Beth had the most difficulty and only offered minimal responses whilst Donald's clarity of speech was the only remaining difficulty which showed up on the Level A assessments.

Whilst verbal dyspraxia is considered to be an expressive language disorder the 5-14 language assessments showed that Beth, Colin and Euan had difficulty with some areas of listening although on the formal receptive language assessments their receptive language scores were within normal limits.

Beth, Colin and Euan had difficulty in the Listening for Information strand at and beyond the 'four information carrying word level'. Listening to information at this level requires that the child is attending, has the memory and the ability to understand vocabulary, concepts and grammatical sequence. The features which constitute the disorder of dyspraxia include poor attentional and sequencing abilities which makes listening in groups difficult. The attainment target *Listening in a Group* expects a response by contributing to the purpose of the activity: this requires that the child not only processes what others are saying but requires an ability to formulate an appropriate response and the confidence and willingness to participate in the group situation.

The four children did less well than their comparison pupils on the reading and writing attainments. As Webster and McConnell (1987) predict:

> Children who come to school with a fluent, sophisticated grasp of spoken language make better all round progress and achieve literacy quicker. Conversely, children who are considered to be immature and restricted in their spoken language abilities, who are unable to absorb through listening for any length of time, will be seriously held back in school.

This appears to be the case for the four children who have a history of immature/deviant phonological systems in that their reading and writing were delayed when compared with their peers. The comparison group was noticeably more confident and capable when presented with unfamiliar books and showed more enthusiasm and ability for the reading and writing tasks. Although Donald and Euan achieved the developmental steps for personal writing they were unable to transfer information from a plan into a piece of functional or imaginative writing. This may be a reflection of their sequencing difficulties but may be because concentration and motor control were expended on drawing up the plan which was required for this task. This is the format of the National Tests for Writing.

Snowling and Stackhouse (1983) found that the dyspraxic child's inability to segment and blend sounds in speech later showed when phonological skills were required for reading and spelling. This, then, must be an area which is targeted jointly by the speech and language therapist and the teacher.

Difficulties common to the language disordered group

The study found that language disordered children present as a group whose language difficulties may appear similar but whose origin have a different basis. The generalisations which can be drawn from the results of the individual case studies are that the younger language disordered children Alan, Beth and Colin are functioning at lower levels of ability than comparison pupils across the four language outcomes and that Donald's, Euan's and Fergus's reading development was delayed and that Donald and Euan were only working towards Level A in writing.

Alan, Beth and Colin have identical profiles for the Reading and Writing outcomes and would be considered as being at the earliest stages of reading development. Difficulty with reading is reflected in the profiles of all the children. Alan was able to read from his 'Link Up' reading book but did not understand all that he read. Fergus was able to read most of the text in the National Reading Test but did not sufficiently understand what he read to pass the test. So all the language disordered group were having difficulty with reading, Alan and Fergus with understanding and Beth, Colin, Donald and Euan with the decoding skills. This difference distinguishes the dyspraxic group from the child with semantic and pragmatic difficulties and the older dysphasic child who had reached a level of decoding language sufficient to read the texts at Level A.

Difficulties were also apparent with the Level A Writing attainment targets. The results of the writing strands showed that the dyspraxic group did less well on the steps of achievement than their comparison group. Alan, who would not be expected to achieve Level A due to his age, had difficulty giving the appropriate information to the teacher to scribe. For the four dyspraxic children the difficulty with writing was mainly one of mastering the technical skills of writing and sentence formation, whilst for the child with semantic and pragmatic difficulties the problem lay with the content of the language which the teacher was to scribe. At the early stages of writing these differences would not be obvious from the results of the attainment targets and need to be made clear in any developmental steps. Children with severe language disorders, such as Fergus, can however, sufficiently master over time, the technical, syntactic and semantic skills necessary to achieve Level A.

Interpretation of English Language 5-14

At the outset of the study it was soon apparent that the teachers and the speech and language therapist had problems with interpretation of the attainment targets when asked to estimate a child's performance at Level A. Some of the attainment targets at Level A were thought to be particularly vague or couched in contradictory language, for example: 'Talk to convey a short, straightforward item of information, an instruction or a direction', gave rise to the following queries: 'What is an item of information?' 'How brief can the item of information be?'

This difficulty with interpretation of the attainment targets is shown by the low percentage of agreement between the estimates of a child's performance and the actual assessment results on the assessment protocol:

- class teachers – 55.4%
- language support teacher – 62.5%
- speech and language therapist – 57.5%

In general the estimates were underestimates of performance. For the three younger children these underestimates were in the Listening and Talking strands as Reading and Writing abilities at the early stage of development were much easier to assess. Underestimates for the three older children were spread across all four outcomes but thirteen out of sixteen overestimates were in Reading.

The study highlighted the difficulty of interpreting English Language 5-14 and raised an awareness that the expectations of the attainment targets at Level A for Listening and Talking were at a much simpler level than the attainment targets at Level A for Reading and Writing. Researchers such as Stackhouse (1989) have found that 'an intact facility for speech and language development appears to be a pre-requisite for satisfactory reading and spelling development'. It could be expected then that the attainment targets for Listening and Talking would contain aspects of receptive and expressive language which involved linguistic skills at a parallel level of ability if not at a more complex level than those required for reading and writing. This would include the ability to understand a sequence of ideas and to recall events in a sequenced order and use a level of syntax at least equivalent to a five year old with an ability to absorb new vocabulary and concepts. However, the following attainment targets in Listening and Talking appear to require only single items of information. For example in the strands:

- *Listening for information, instructions and directions,* the attainment target states: 'Listen to a short straight forward text which gives an item of information, instruction or direction, and show that they understand, and, where appropriate, can use what has been heard.'

- *Conveying information instruction and directions,* the attainment target states: 'Talk to convey a short item of information, an instruction or a direction.'

Reference is made in both of these attainment targets to just one item of information and there are no guidelines for what this should entail. So minimal responses often produced by language disordered children could score as highly as a more complex response. This does not seem a realistic level of requirement considering the type of sentence structure expected by such schemes as the Derbyshire Language Scheme at the four year level or by Crystal's Language Assessment and Remediation Procedures (LARSP). Level B attainment targets require *items* of information.

Again, in the Level A strands:

- *Listening in order to respond to texts,* the attainment target states: 'Listen to a simple story, poem or dramatic text, and respond in a way that shows some reaction to one aspect of it.'

- *Talking about texts,* the attainment target states: 'Talk about a simple story, poem or dramatic text that has been heard or read, revealing some reaction to one aspect of it.'

Both these attainment targets require some reaction to one aspect of a story. Again as there are no guidelines to what type of reaction, this again could be a minimal response which may be mainly irrelevant to the main part of the story. The Reading strand *Reading to reflect on the writer's ideas and craft* is perhaps a more realistic requirement for Level A and goes beyond the Listening and Talking attainments in that it involves discussion and the ability to extract an important idea. The attainment target states:

- 'Read and with teacher support, talk about a short, straightforward text showing that they understand one important idea.'

Differences in expectations can also be found between the Reading and Writing attainment targets and the requirements of the Reading and Writing National Tests at Level A which are more demanding. For example, the Reading

Narrative Test, *The Lighthouse Keeper's Lunch*, requires that the child reads reasonably independently in order to get the main ideas of the story, answers an oral question and then completes two activities which involve using the information from the text to sequence the plot of the story and match up labels with the appropriate picture.

The criteria for attaining Level A in the National Test for imaginative writing allow some teacher help but require the child to:

- convey some sense of what happens;
- include a short narrative sequence;
- include two or three linked details or events.

These expectations (which should be age appropriate as they were piloted before being used in the 1991-1992 National Tests), demand a great deal more than the one item pieces of information required for the Listening and Talking attainment targets at Level A. This suggests that either the Listening and Talking attainment targets are not sufficiently developed or the National Tests for Level A are too difficult. This is of course assuming that Level A is a parallel level across the four outcomes.

The finding that the Listening and Talking attainment targets expect less than the Reading and Writing attainment targets make it all the more important to have clearly defined stages or steps of development within the Listening and Talking outcomes which bear a relationship to the level of skills required for Reading and Writing. A child who achieves the present Level A attainment in Talking would not necessarily need to be able to communicate in sentences and therefore it would be unrealistic to expect Level A work in Reading and Writing. Whilst it is acknowledged that children will progress at different rates across the language outcomes the imbalance between the Listening and Talking, and the Reading and Writing strands further complicates the assessment procedure and leads to confusion. A parent of a language disordered child who has achieved Level A in Listening and Talking, may assume that their child's language difficulties in these areas are no longer cause for concern.

Conclusion

English Language 5-14 was not only difficult to interpret as it contained insufficient detail to give a clear understanding of what should be achieved at Level A but there was no way of monitoring early language development which is necessary for the language disordered child. However, it is possible that those who compiled this document were assuming that children had already reached a certain level of linguistic competence by school age. It has also heightened awareness of the importance of developing listening and talking skills for the development of reading and writing and this has implications for the balance of the curriculum for language disordered children to be weighted initially towards developing these skills.

The strands in the framework of English Language 5-14 provide aspects of listening, talking, reading and writing which should be included in the language disordered child's curriculum. To use these strands realistic steps of achievement need to be included in some format as the attainment targets at Level A are too vague and unspecific. The assessment protocol developed for this study was an attempt to develop the 5-14 English Language framework by including steps into each attainment target which gave information on the quality and quantity of the child's linguistic competence which was not available from the A, WTA or NRA marking of the criteria for achieving Level A.

These steps in the assessment protocol were only broad indicators of difficulties. So when a step indicated that the child had difficulty with syntax, grammatical analysis would then be required to analyse the extent of the problem.

The results of the research posed the problem of how to proceed. It was clear that English Language 5-14 lacked information on the criteria for achieving Level A, especially in the Listening and Talking outcomes. The assessment protocol with its additional steps of development went some way to showing the differences in language performance but whether the developmental progression contained sufficient detail to be useful to other teachers of language impaired pupils would need to be investigated.

An alternative to using the type of format presented in this study would be to add a specific section or sections under the broad heading of communication skills which would include aspects of functional communication (pragmatics), syntax, semantics (including vocabulary and concepts), phonology and articulation. Such sections could be used when a child was identified as having a specific difficulty in one of these areas.

This study was an attempt to transfer the type of detailed information which is gained from specialist speech and language assessments and schemes of work into the framework of English Language 5-14 which in its present format is vague and lacks cohesion. If English Language 5-14 is to be used for planning, evaluating and assessing English Language for language disordered children, realistic stages of development need to be incorporated into the framework. It is important to find a way of communicating the detailed and specific information gained from the language assessments carried out by speech and language therapists and specialist language teachers to teachers and parents in non-threatening language which can also be related to the child's progress through the curriculum. English Language 5-14 provides a potential framework for professionals and parents to work together but requires a great deal of clarification as well as very specific development of the Listening and Talking strands in the early stage.

References

Bishop, D. and Rosenbloom, L. (1987) Childhood language disorders: classification and overview. In *Language Development and Disorders,* eds. W. Yule and M. Rutter. Oxford, MacKeith Press

Bryant, P. E. and Bradley, L. (1985) *Children's Reading Problems.* Oxford, Blackwell

Byers-Brown, B. and Edwards, M. (1989) *Developmental Disorders of Language.* London, Whurr

Crystal, D., Fletcher, P. and Garman, M. (1989) *Grammatical Analysis of Language Disability.* London, Whurr

Garton, A. and Pratt, C. (1989) *The Development of Spoken and Written Language.* Oxford, Basil Blackwell

Knowles, W. and Masidlover, M. (1982) *Derbyshire Language Scheme.* Derbyshire County Council

Locke, A. and Beech, M. (1991) *Teaching Talking.* Windsor, NFER Nelson

Prout, L. M. (1992) 'The Assessment of Oral Language in Children with Reading and Spelling Difficulties'. Unpublished paper presented at the conference on 'Children with Language Difficulties, Reading and Spelling Problems', Newcastle University, April 1992

Scottish Office Education Department. (1991) *Curriculum and Assessment in Scotland. National Guidelines: English Language 5-14.* Edinburgh, HMSO

Snowling, M. and Stackhouse, J. (1983) Spelling performance of children with developmental verbal dyspraxia. *Developmental Medicine and Child Neurology.* **25**, 430-7

Stackhouse, J. (1989) Relationship between spoken and written language disorders. In *Child Language Disability, Implications in an Educational Setting,* eds. K. Mogford and J. Sadler. Clevedon, Multilingual Matters Ltd

Webster, A. and V. (1991) *Profiles of the Language Impaired.* Bristol, Avec Designs Ltd

Webster, A. and McConnell, C. (1987) *Special Needs in Ordinary Schools: Children with Speech and Language Difficulties.* London, Cassell

Appendix

The following diagrams show the results of the Level A attainment targets for the language disordered children and their comparison groups.

Key:

Outcome	***LISTENING***
STRAND 1	Listening for information, instructions and directions
STRAND 2	Listening in groups
STRAND 3	Listening in order to respond to texts
STRAND 4	Awareness of genre
Outcome	***TALKING***
STRAND 1	Conveying information, instructions and directions
STRAND 2	Talking in groups
STRAND 3	Talking about experiences, feelings and opinions
STRAND 4	Talking about texts
STRAND 5	Audience awareness
Outcome	***READING***
STRAND 1	Reading for information
STRAND 2	Reading for enjoyment
STRAND 3	Reading to reflect on the writer's ideas and craft
STRAND 4	Awareness of genre
STRAND 5	Reading aloud
Outcome	***WRITING***
STRAND 1	Functional writing
STRAND 2	Personal writing
STRAND 3	Imaginative writing
STRAND 4	Punctuation and structure
STRAND 5	Spelling
STRAND 6	Handwriting and presentation

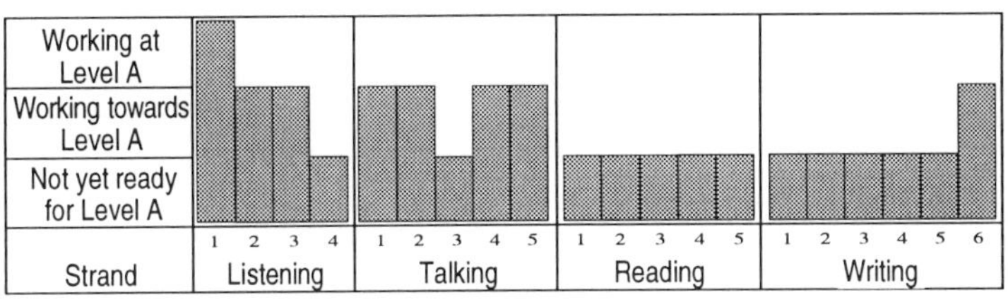

Alan

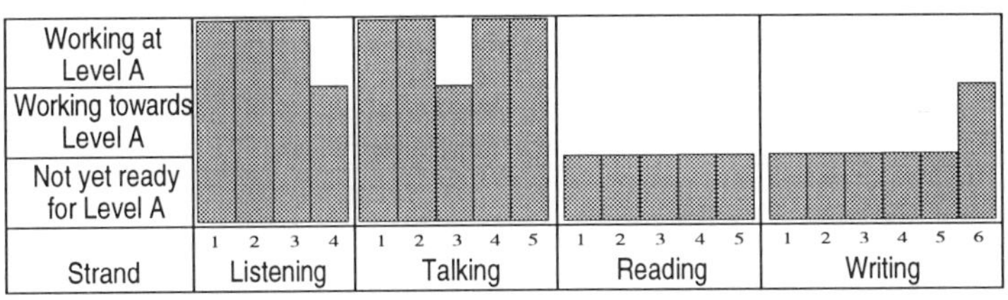

C1 & C2 (identical)

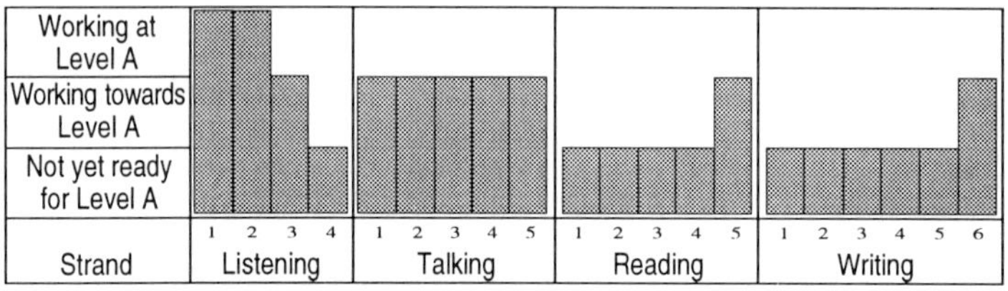

Beth

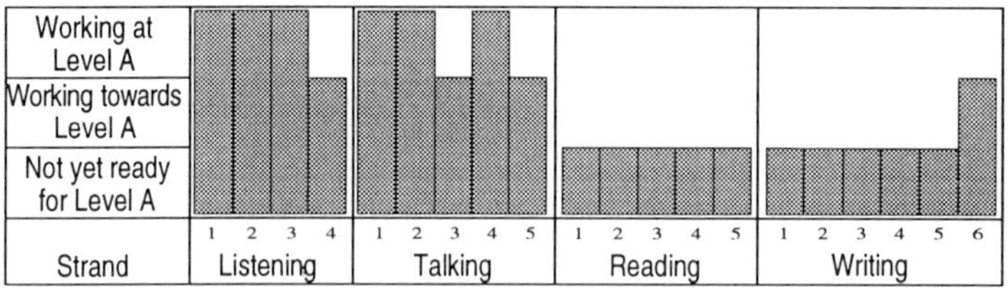

Colin

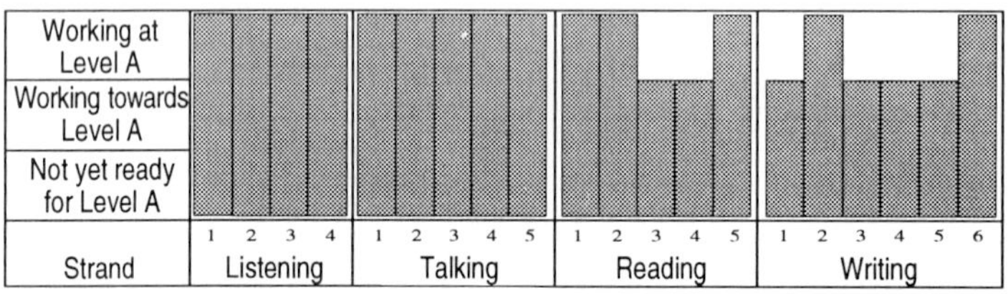

C3

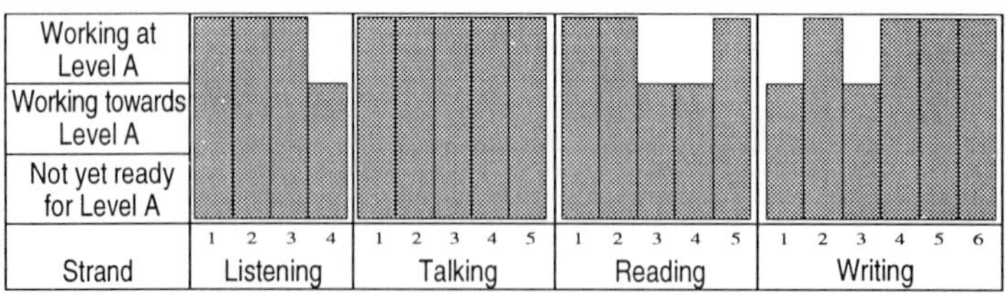

C4

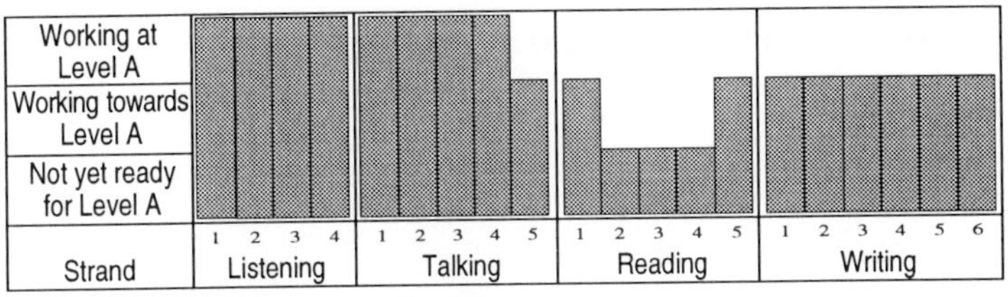

Donald

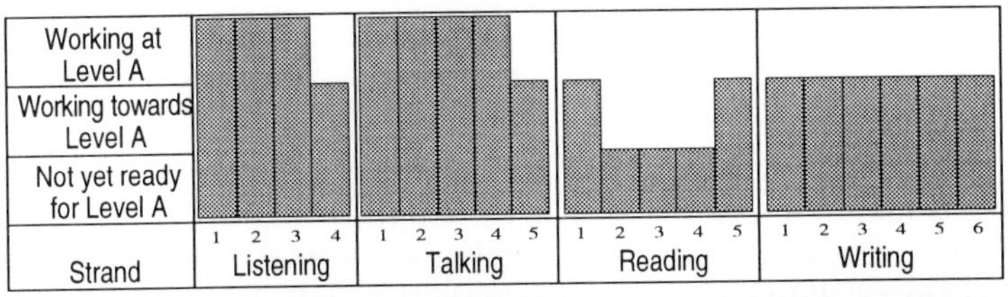

Euan

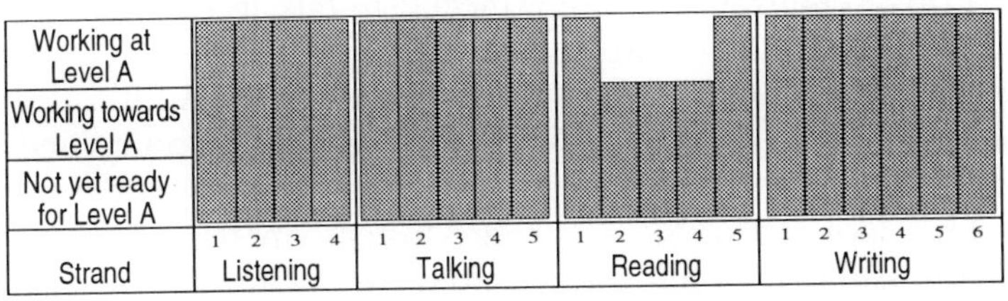

Fergus

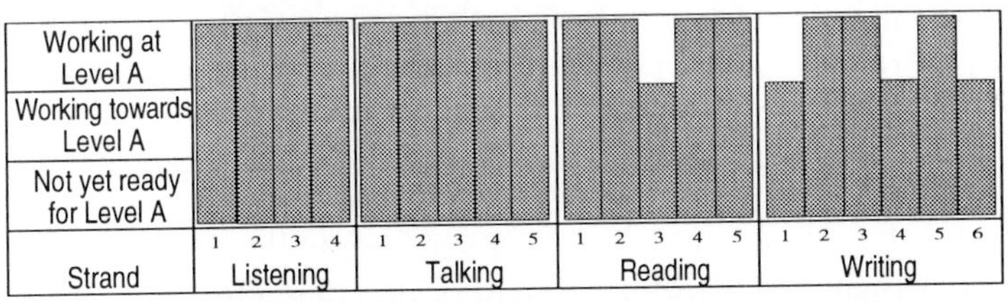

C5

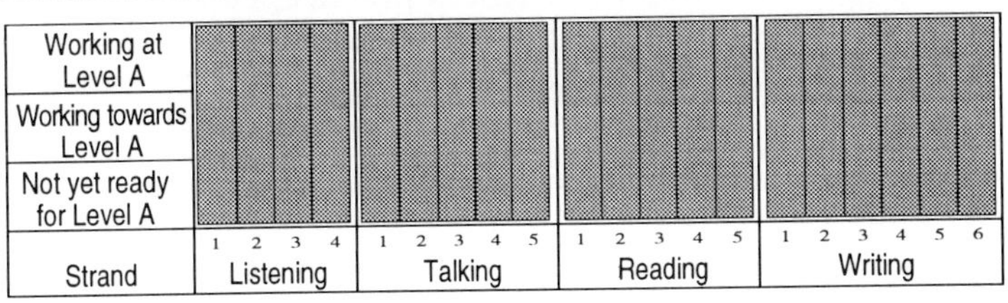

C6

Reluctant Talkers in the Early Years: some key issues

Edward Jefferies and Sally Dolan

Introduction

The 5-14 English language guidelines (SOED, 1991a) identify the development of skill in talking as a major aim of teaching in the English language area and there is little need to justify research with a focus on talking in general. A particular area of interest is how those children who are reluctant to talk in class can be enabled to work towards the attainment outcomes for talking at Level A. A small-scale study was therefore carried out as part of the SOED/Regional Authorities Practice Development Initiative for educational psychologists specifically concerned with this aspect of the challenge that teachers face in implementing the guidelines.

It is most important to look at how skill in talking is fostered in the early years at school because this is presumably when attitudes towards talking are formed. It is also clear from the researches of Wells (1985) and Tizard and Hughes (1984) that, while most children come to school with a strong command of oral language, many do not use this capability in the public and formal setting of the classroom.

In response to this perceived deficiency there are teaching programmes and advice available on encouraging oracy amongst young children (cf Tann, 1991). However, there is also evidence (e.g. Edwards and Mercer, 1987) that patterns of language use in classrooms are not in a simple sense deficient. Rather, the way in which language is used reflects both the realities of teaching children in groups and the deeply embedded ideas which underlie teachers' practice. This means that some issues in relation to talking can only be addressed by looking at the overall approach and the interactional style which teachers adopt.

The research method which was adopted was to observe teachers in action in their own classrooms. Such a form of research ought to make use of the knowledge which teachers have acquired about how classrooms work. A collaborative model of research was, therefore, employed in which the teachers' insights into their own practice formed part of the data.

Aim

The aim of the research was to identify factors which are important in encouraging children to talk in a public and open way in early education. It looked at talking in whole class situations and in small groups with the teacher present. Informal talk amongst children in groups where there was no teacher present was not considered, despite its importance.

Method

The research was carried out in six primary schools normally visited by the two psychologists working on the project. In each school the head teacher was asked to identify an appropriate P2 class. Headteachers were unlikely to suggest teachers about whose practice they were concerned; it is therefore fair to conclude that the sample was of competent practitioners. (All the classes appeared well organised and purposeful and the behaviour of the children was beyond reproach.) The schools selected were located in the east and the west of Glasgow serving catchment areas which varied, although none had a significant middle-class component.

Within each class, the teacher was asked to identify, by first name only, the four children who were the least likely to talk in the normal course of events. The selection was made irrespective of the children's performance in other respects. The children selected included some who were above average in reading and mathematics as well as some whose overall attainments were limited. Children for whom English was a second language were not included. Collectively, these children will be referred to as the 'target' children.

The standard method for recording classroom language in detail has been the use of audio-taping. Small cassette recorders with tie-clip microphones were attached to the teacher. These successfully picked up the language used in the teacher's presence (cf. Jefferies, unpublished, for a technical discussion). Each tape was transcribed.

Various methods of complementing the taped record with a behavioural account were considered and video-taping was selected. Although the presence of the camera made it difficult for the teacher to react naturally to being observed, a video tape has the advantages that its permanence allows it to be re-analysed and its richness allows the fine detail of interactions to be examined. Its greatest advantage was that it made it possible to discuss the observations with the teachers after the event. An observer was also needed to identify those occasions on which the target children spoke. Both researchers were, therefore, involved in each school.

An appointment was made, generally about two weeks after the data-gathering, to discuss the transcripts and the video-taped observations with the teacher. The primary focus of this discussion was those factors which encouraged talk from the target children, although, inevitably, it became more general.

Although the presence of the observers obviously affected the behaviour of the teachers this was not necessarily a great problem. The researchers asked the teachers to maintain their normal class routine while working in a way which would encourage the less verbal children to talk. The data which were gathered do not therefore claim to be representative of everyday practice in these classrooms. Instead, they are a record of the approach that six teachers took to the challenge of encouraging some children to talk more freely. Each teacher had a different set of children in a different school. Each chose to work on a different topic.

A categorisation system was developed for comparing the observations in one class with those in the others. The system developed and the observations made in each class are fully discussed in Jefferies and Dolan (forthcoming). By making systematic comparisons amongst classes it was possible to identify some key issues in encouraging reluctant talkers, all of whom were at a pre-Level A stage in their talking skills. This paper looks at each of these issues in turn and illustrates the questions it raises by means of extracts from the transcripts of the observations carried out in the six classes.

Encouraging reluctant talkers

Given the aim of the study, the first question to be addressed is whether there are specific, identifiable ways of interacting with reluctant talkers which encourage them to talk.

Overwhelmingly, talk in the six classrooms followed a pattern with three components:

- teacher initiates
- child responds
- teacher reacts to the child's response.

Over 90% of interactions overall followed this pattern. A natural question to ask is therefore whether one form of teacher initiation produced more response from the target children than another. This question has to be approached with great caution here; critical variables, above all the verbal skills of the target children, were uncontrolled. It is also the case that there were substantial differences in the amount of talk overall amongst the six classes, which might result from factors such as personal teaching style or whole school ethos which were not studied.

Bearing these qualifications in mind, it is possible to look at some results as suggestive of a trend. The mean length of utterance in words which the children produced in response to each category of teacher initiation identified during the analysis of the transcripts is shown in Figure 8.1.

The limited length of the talk prompted by the first two categories of initiation suggests that children are likely to have less to say where the discussion focuses on immediate materials. A typical example might be this section of

Fig. 8.1: Length of child utterances in response to types of teacher initiation

Type of initiation	Mean length in words of child's utterance
Questions on the overt content of the material used (e.g. books, play materials)	2.4
Questions on the implicit content of the material used	3.3
Asking children to project into situations or predict outcomes	2.3
Asking children to recall personal experiences	5.1
Asking children to give information or knowledge from outwith class	3.2
Asking children to give an opinion	6.8
Asking children to clarify what they have said	5.1
Offering children an opportunity to contribute	6.1

dialogue amongst a group of children and their teacher in relation to a reading book which they were discussing before they read it. (Only the target children are named, using fictitious names; other children are identified as Child.)

Teacher: ... Right let's look at the picture on the front cover. Where is the witch?
Child: On a broom.
Teacher: She's on her broom. What's she doing?
Child: She's flying.
Teacher: She's flying. What's she flying over?
Child: A house.
Teacher: Well, there's a house in the picture. Colin?
Colin: Trees.

This contrasts with a section later in the same transcript where the teacher is asking the children to relate the witch's flying to their own experiences:

Teacher: ... Anyone else been on an aeroplane?
Child: When I went to eh eh a park. I don't know the park's name. And when I went to the park there was a big helicopter. And you, and on the, it's one pound to get a shot, going like that (demonstrates) fast and you can see everything. You can see your mum and all that.

This observation runs counter to one of the orthodoxies of early education; that young children need concrete, visible support for their learning. The limitations of this orthodoxy are discussed by Egan (1988). The fact that, in general, these children spoke at greater length when they were recounting 'stories' of their own experiences lends some support to Egan's emphasis on the primacy of the narrative mode of learning.

It may appear obvious that questions about overt content will produce limited responses but it is also true where children are asked to work out ideas which are implicit in the content of the materials which are to hand. For example, in a different class where the children were listening to a story about a child being unwell the following exchange occurred:

Teacher:	... What's the mum doing, Gemma?
Gemma:	Reading a story.
Teacher:	She's reading him a story. Isn't she. Is he enjoying it? How do you know he's enjoying it, Christopher?
Child:	Cause he's laughing.
Teacher:	He's laughing and what did his sister do, Gary? What's she bringing him?
Gary:	A teddy.
Teacher:	A teddy. And what's the teddy going to do?
Gary:	Listen.

Asked about their own experiences the children again responded at greater length:

Child:	Well, a long time ago at the doctor's I got a jag.
Teacher:	You got a jag.
Child:	And I had to go to bed at the same time.
Teacher:	You had to go to bed as well. What about you, David?
David:	I was sick for two full days and my ma had to call the doctor and she had to go into my next door neighbour's because she doesn't have a phone.

Interestingly, when teachers asked children to project themselves into a situation or to predict what would happen next the children responded with a similar lack of elaboration. Perhaps it is the case that this cognitively challenging form of talking is fairly difficult for young children. (Of course, this is not intended to be an argument against asking P2s to engage in prediction or projection, it is an observation that doing so may not offer them an opportunity for talking at any length.)

A typical example of talking involving projection comes from a class working on a topic called 'Fantasy Island':

Teacher:	Right we could have news about someone falling in the water. Now who would it be? Would it be a child or an adult?
Children:	An adult.
Teacher:	An adult And would it be one of the islanders or a visitor?
Children:	A visitor.
Teacher:	A visitor. Right so a visitor is going to fall in the water. Why? What's happened? Have you got any idea, Derek?
Derek:	It was a boat.
Teacher:	He was out in a boat. Why did he go out in a boat?
Derek:	To catch some fish.

Children are clearly able to project themselves into an imagined situation. However where the projection is constrained, in this case, by the need to develop a coherent story they are challenged cognitively in a way which may restrict their use of language. A contrasting projection was the account given by one child of a hill walk he had carried out at the weekend.

Alexander	I had to get a big stick to climb up it.
Teacher:	Did you it was so high.
Alexander:	Yes.
Teacher:	And what could you see from the top of your hill?
Alexander:	Em I could see up in England it was so bright.
Teacher:	Has anyone got a question for him about that?
Child:	Did you like it?
Alexander:	Yes.
Teacher:	What did you like about it?
Alexander:	Rolling down the hill. Then when I got up I did a fifteen feet jump back up in the air.
Teacher:	Where was the mountain?
Alexander:	It was at the fish farm.
Teacher:	So it was in the countryside?
Alexander:	Yes, and a bull chased after me.
Teacher:	A bull chased after you. I bet you got a fright.
Alexander:	Yes I was running as fast as I could...When the bull was running after me I was laughing.
Teacher:	Were you? But did you manage to run when you were laughing?
Alexander:	Yes... I managed to jump over a fence.

This story was clearly a mixture of fact and projection and it raises questions of the need for relevance in classroom talk, an issue to be considered in the next section. However, it is important to bear in mind that Alexander was one of the reluctant talkers and that, for him, a sustained flow of language like this was a rare occurrence.

It therefore appears that less constrained types of initiation, offering children an opportunity to contribute their own information or opinions, offer better opportunities for extended responses. However, the implications of this are not as simple as they might appear to be. Talk is the main medium through which teachers communicate with the children in their classes; its character is therefore central to the texture of classroom life. How a teacher talks with his or her pupils does not reduce to questioning skills. Instead it is inextricably entwined in the pedagogy which underlies all of his or her teaching. It is necessary, therefore, to look at issues at a deeper level than the surface of teacher initiations.

Control

The question of who controls the agenda for talking is at the heart of how teachers talk with children and it explains many of its characteristics. Classrooms have to be controlled settings or no-one is able to learn. The teacher's main medium for exercising control is talking. It is therefore critical to teachers to retain control over what is said. At home, or in the playground, most children would expect to initiate talk, determine the subject matter and play a reciprocal role; this is not their expectation in class.

The feature of the talk observed in these six classes, which distinguishes it from all other forms of talk in its lack of reciprocity, is the predominance of direct questioning. This finding is a central one of considerable significance. It is clear that the primary method by which these six teachers encouraged the reluctant talkers to contribute was by directing questions to them. Further, the teachers did not in general use a neutral form of questioning which encouraged a variety of responses. Teaching itself is always carried out with an aim in mind so that teachers' talk tends to have an aim in mind. An example is this sequence concerning baking:

Teacher:	... How many people have helped their mum to bake something in the house? before you start you have to go and collect things, don't you. What kind of things would you have to collect?
Child:	Dough.
Teacher:	Well, you have to make the dough. What do you need to make the dough? Angela?
Angela:	*no response*
Teacher:	Have you helped your mummy to bake in the house?
Angela:	No.

Teacher:	Have you seen your mummy baking? (Right, can you leave those things alone just now). What kind of things would she need?
Child:	*indecipherable* of sausages.
Teacher:	Well, if she's making a pie.
Child:	Eggs.
Teacher:	Eggs.
Child:	Tomatoes.
Teacher:	Just leave it just now, Peter.
Child:	My mum puts tomatoes in the oven.
Teacher:	Oh right, maybe tomatoes. But if she was baking a cake what's the main thing that she would need, Andrew?
Andrew:	Chocolate.
Teacher:	Well that would be to put on top of it maybe.
Child	Em, the ingre...
Teacher:	She'd need a bag of... I don't think you'd be much help in the house baking. She'd need some flour, wouldn't she?

Perhaps the most significant feature of this exchange is the fact that the general concept of 'ingredients' which could have organised much of the thinking here gets lost as the teacher pursues her objective of getting someone to say the word 'flour'.

It is possible for teachers to surrender control of the agenda temporarily and the example of Alexander's hill walk in the previous section was an occasion on which this occurred. The control which teachers have to maintain need not be absolute. Equally, the freedom has to be limited; all the teachers pointed out that some children will talk at great length about their current interests but these interests are often not germane to the classroom. Criteria of relevance are needed but, just as with children's writing, there is a balance to be struck at the early stages between encouraging all efforts and promoting relevance.

Clearly, the response that anyone gets from his or her interlocutors is a major factor in determining how much he or she is willing to say. Teachers have therefore to judge their responses carefully if they want to encourage children to talk. A very common pattern is for the teacher to acknowledge the child's response in prefacing or framing the next question. An example is from a lesson in which talk was concerned with words beginning with /gl/:

Child:	Glitter.
Teacher:	Glitter. What's glitter like? Where would you see glitter at this time of the year? We send them. You get them every morning.

Child:	Cards.
Teacher:	And what's on the cards a lot of the time?

This sort of response offers feedback to the child on the acceptability of his or her response. The feedback is most direct when the teacher repeats what the child has said by echoing or expanding. This was the second most common way for teachers to respond to a child and its frequency marks classroom interaction out from everyday discourse. It appears to serve several functions; to make sure that other children hear what is said, to confirm the validity of the child's contribution and to retain control of the dialogue in the teacher's hands.

Purpose

It was obvious from the follow up discussions that for the teachers talking was, in the main, an end in itself. It was equally obvious that this purpose was at most an implicit one for the children. Young as they are, P2 children know that they go to school to learn to read, to write and to count and, more widely, to learn about the world in which they live; few would consider learning to talk as an end of their schooling. With one exception, talking was always embedded in another activity so that it was ostensibly incidental to the purpose of the lesson. Consequently, the children must have had a different view of the purpose of the activity from the teacher.

One typical example of how purposes are not made explicit can be found in this transition from a point about phonics (the 'j' sound that 'g' makes in some contexts) to reminiscences about a visit to the zoo:

Teacher:	... Any other words that we did?
Child:	Giraffe.
Teacher:	Giraffe, right. Now I'm going to write this down for you. An 'i' makes a 'g' say 'j'. Giraffe (writes on blackboard). Now I wonder, do you remember we went to the zoo last year? You remember we all got on the bus and we had fun and we went to the zoo. And we saw so many different animals, do you remember? Now did we see a giraffe at the zoo?

The times at which the purposes for talk were probably most apparent to the children were those in which talking was an ancillary activity. An obvious example is when a teacher introduced a new reading book by looking at some of the pictures and discussing them. Talking may well have been seen here by the children as a preliminary to serious schoolwork rather than as a skill to be developed in its own right. A parallel example occurred when a teacher talked about the pictures on a worksheet, elaborating on school sports and what detectives did before the children undertook the mathematics task which was its ostensible purpose. Similarly, one teacher prepared the children for a writing task by talking about what they might write.

The example of talking in preparation for writing indicates quite clearly that talking in preparation for another activity is an entirely appropriate procedure and often essential. However, if this is the main role that talking fulfils it would be surprising if the children did not regard talking itself as a preparatory exercise.

Contexts for talking

Talking always takes place in a context of other learning and for all of the teachers it was important that it should be integrated into the ongoing work of the class. There were obvious examples where this was the case: on three occasions talk was part of work related to a reading book or reading skills such as phonics; in two classes the talk was related to a theme which had integrated the work of the class for some time.

However, it was not apparent that the most integrated parts of the work observed were the ones in which talk flowed most freely; the examples of talking focused on the material visible to both teacher and pupil already given illustrate this point.

The liveliest and most fluent exchanges probably occurred at times where the content bore no relation to the ongoing work of the class. In fact there is a suspicion that where talk is too well integrated, that is, where it covers content which the teacher and the children have already shared, the teacher has to make strenuous efforts at keeping the discussion alive. Examples can be seen in this discussion of the class visit to the zoo:

Teacher:	Can you tell me something, Mark, that was special about the rhinoceros?
Mark:	They were big.
Teacher:	They were big. Did they look frightening or would you have wanted to jump in beside them and speak to them?
Mark:	No... Cause they'd kill you.
Teacher:	Were they big fat animals or were they tall thin animals like the giraffe?
Mark:	Big and fat.
Teacher:	What can you tell me about its skin?
Mark:	Smooth.
Teacher:	It was smooth? But we never had a chance to feel it. Do you think it was smooth?

The second context for talk, one which was mentioned by all the teachers, is that of the emotional climate within which talk takes place. Any child will be reluctant to talk if they feel exposed and some children feel exposed in almost all classroom situations. The contrasting comments of two of the teachers indicate the dilemma in which teachers find themselves. One teacher emphasised that it is reluctant talkers who are most in need of developing these skills, while the other pointed out the risk of increasing, or even creating, a fear of talking in public. Teachers' differing perspectives on this dilemma may explain why there were considerable differences in the overall amount of talk in different classes.

Grouping

One aspect of the context in which talking takes place is that of the nature and size of the group of children involved. All the teachers identified group dynamics and the effect of more talkative children on the willingness of others to contribute as a key factor when considering reluctant talkers. In the main, teachers used existing language groups, but two teachers formed groups especially for the purpose of the observation, in one case explicitly aiming to provide a balance of fluent and reluctant talkers. In one group the boys did appear to dominate the conversation but in the other five there was no very obvious sex difference.

The effect that large numbers have on the context for talking both emotionally and numerically appears obvious. It offers a justification for seeing small groups as a better context for talking than whole classes, a view supported by the 5-14 English language guidelines at Level A and by four out of the six teachers here. However, the evidence of this study is equivocal on this point. Two of the teachers worked with whole class groups for the majority of the hour. One teacher worked with the whole class for approximately half of the hour. The three others did not have the whole class together at all. Where teachers split their classes, the size of the group with which they worked varied between twelve and six. Only one worked with a very small group, of four. No-one worked with an individual.

The overall quantity of talk observed from the target children in each class did not bear an obvious relationship to the size of group. In one whole class lesson sheer numbers did appear to limit the opportunity for any individual to talk , but the observations made in another class suggests that these factors can be overcome. Assumptions about grouping are part of the received wisdom of 'good primary practice' made problematic by work such as that of Alexander (1992) who summarises the evidence on the effects of grouping in the following way: 'Whatever the interpretation, the cumulative research and survey data since 1978 suggests an urgent need to look at the justifications, dynamics and effectiveness of grouping.'

It appears that group size interacts with factors like purpose and interactional style rather than offering a solution to the 'problems' of class teaching. The following sequence occurred in a whole class context but it was quite clear to the child that she had a purpose of telling the other children something about a book which she had read. Significantly, the teacher involved the other children in this purpose.

Teacher:	Is there anything you'd like to ask Linda about her book? Any questions you've got?
Child:	Did you like it?
Linda:	Yes, there's a lot of colours and people painting with bright paints, different paints.
Child:	Which bit did you like the best?
Linda:	That one.
Teacher:	You like that one. Why do you like that one?
Linda:	Because it had good pictures and it gave you the idea of it...
Child:	Where did you get the book?
Linda:	I sent away for it, for another book. Can't remember what it was. And you couldn't get the other book so they sent me this and I got the *indecipherable* book.

Conclusions

Two separate reasons can be distinguished for emphasising the importance of talking. In the first place, the skills which make up oracy are important in their own right and, it is widely argued, neglected in school (MacLure et al., 1988; Tarelton, 1988). In particular, young children and children who have learning difficulties are unlikely to derive maximum benefit from education if they lack skill in this primary area (Hutchcroft, 1992).

The other important role that talking plays is that it is one of the major means by which enquiry can be conducted. Talking in a range of classroom contexts offers children an opportunity to explore ideas with others, both their peers and their teachers. It is therefore an essential tool for learning in every area of the curriculum. The fact that teachers who were asked to concentrate on talking chose to carry out, in the main, lessons very firmly in the English language area of the curriculum is given added significance by the fact that talking is located in this area in the 5-14 programme. This runs the risk that talking becomes a skill to be developed without reference to what is being talked about.

The distinct roles of talking appeared to be integrated with one another in much of the talking which was observed. This is probably because at the early stages of education high value is attached to the provision of an integrated curriculum which is not arbitrarily divided into subjects or skills. However, one effect of this philosophy may be to make it difficult for children to know what is expected of them. All the teachers had clear objectives for the work which they undertook during the time when they were observed and they all had clear aims in relation to developing the skills of talking. Nevertheless, in practice, the purpose for talking was often obscure to an outside observer and rarely made explicit to the children.

Similarly, in providing a rounded, natural curriculum teachers endeavour to keep talking informal, acting as if it arose in the normal course of events. This may serve to increase the uncertainty of purpose. All the teachers were highly skilled at keeping the talk flowing but they did so by means of controlling and shaping the conversation, so that instead of dialogue there was pseudo dialogue. Children inevitably recognise that classroom talk has its own rules and conventions so that the value which is attached to informality and naturalness may be misplaced. The skills being learned in school are not the skills of everyday conversation. Talking in school cannot replicate the richness and shared reference which Tizard and Hughes (1984) note in talk at home, so that as conversation it is inescapably impoverished.

There are talking skills which children can learn in school but not at home; those of exposition, explanation, audience awareness and all the other skills of public talking. It was observed that P2 children can successfully manage tasks in which they are expected to speak to an audience and engage in a dialogue with that audience. There is, therefore, a clear place for talking as part of skills development in English language. Not only the teacher, but also the children should be aware that there are distinct times at which the object of their work in class is to talk as well and as interestingly as possible. Children are more likely to talk at length if they are genuinely engaged in sharing experiences or communicating information that is genuinely new to their audience. This means that teachers have also to face the challenge of allowing children to set some of the agenda for classroom talk.

Every skill which is promoted in English language work is developed in and transferred to other areas of the curriculum and talking is no different from reading or writing in this respect. While there are specific skills which can be located in English language teaching, talk will often arise most usefully as part of enquiry in areas of the curriculum with well-defined content. Talking is given a central place in several curricular areas in the 5-14 guidelines. One instance is in problem solving and enquiry in mathematics where an example is given of how a mathematical task may be explored:

> The class is going to hold a birthday party for one of their number. *In the course of a discussion led by the teacher* the pupils will have to make decisions about who will sit at each table; the amount of food, cups, straws, etc. needed; how the food can be shared fairly; how to make sure nobody is left out (SOED, 1991b, emphasis added).

The converse of the preceding comments about talking as part of English language is that in such situations talking *is* incidental, it is a tool for learning and children will understand this purpose. At such times teachers have to set the agenda and criteria of relevance have to be applied, flexibly.

In observing their work and talking to teachers it is quite apparent that talk is highly valued and strongly promoted. Equally, there are no grounds for complacency. The traditional reticence of the Scot may have its origins in wider aspects of our culture but it is all too easy for these to be reinforced in our schools.

Improving talking in the early years

Rightly, hard pressed teachers would welcome suggestions for activities which will assist children in working towards the talking attainment outcome at Level A. It is true that some conclusions can be drawn about approaches which are likely to engage children in talking rather than second guessing teachers. However, the preceding discussion should have made it clear that superficial adjustments to classroom activities are unlikely to address the question. Equally, the view that 'talking is what we do in the infants', expressed by one teacher, needs to be refined and developed.

As well as opportunities to hone their skills in facilitating, commenting and questioning, teachers need opportunities to examine the underlying assumptions that they bring to talking. Appropriate staff development opportunities would allow teachers to observe other practitioners in action, probably on video, followed by structured discussion of the key practice issues such as those of grouping and control. It would also consider ways in which children can be encouraged to share in setting the agenda for talking. Perhaps most importantly there is a need to think about disentangling the purposes of talking so that skill in talking is not viewed as acquired incidentally or as a by-product of the rest of the curriculum but as something to be developed in its own right.

References

Alexander, R. (1992) *Policy and Practice in Primary Education*. London, Routledge

Edwards, D. and Mercer, M. (1987) *Common Knowledge*. London, Methuen

Egan, K. (1988) *Teaching as Storytelling*. London, Routledge

Hutchcroft, D. (1992) The primacy of talk. In *Learning Difficulties in Primary Classrooms: Delivering the Whole Curriculum,* eds. K. Jones, and T. Charlton. London, Routledge

Jefferies, E. (unpublished) 'Pre-five Services and Children with Disabilities'. Ph.D. thesis, University of Glasgow

Jefferies, E. and Dolan, S. (forthcoming) Talking and reluctant talkers in infant classrooms. In *Practice Development Initiatives 1992-1993*. SOED/Regional Psychological Services

Maclure, M., Phillips, T. and Wilkinson, A. (1988) *Oracy Matters*. Buckingham, Open University Press

Scottish Office Education Department. (1991a) *Curriculum and Assessment in Scotland. National Guidelines: English Language 5-14*. Edinburgh, HMSO

Scottish Office Education Department. (1991b) *Curriculum and Assessment in Scotland. National Guidelines: Mathematics 5-14*. Edinburgh, HMSO

Tann, S. (1991) *Developing Language in the Primary Classroom.* London, Cassell

Tarelton, R. (1988) *Learning and Talking: A Practical Guide to Oracy across the Curriculum.* London, Routledge

Tizard, B. and Hughes, M. (1984) *Young Children Learning*. London, Fontana

Wells, G. (1985) *Language Development in the Pre-School Years*. Cambridge, Cambridge University Press

Quite a Case: a multidisciplinary approach to a complex, expressive language problem and its implications for literacy

Mo Townson and Margaret McGregor

This chapter is the result of a joint effort to meet the needs of one small – very active – five year old, who communicated successfully with his peers but was totally unintelligible to the adult world. His early meetings with authority figures suggested that he had many strengths but needed a great deal of support to overcome his difficulties.

Case-study

Mike was born the second child of young parents, his sister was sixteen months his senior. Pregnancy and delivery were normal but he was an 'irritable baby' with early feeding problems. He sucked readily but did not co-ordinate sucking and swallowing and choked easily. Asthma was diagnosed at three months and he attended the asthma clinic regularly including several spells as an in-patient. Medication was prescribed and by the time he was three years old his asthma was well controlled. He sat at five months, walked at ten months and babbled freely but speech was slow to develop. He was an active child with no fear of danger, and his very lively behaviour was thought to be a result of his early medication. Family reports however state that his father at the same age showed similar behaviour patterns.

He was referred for a speech and language assessment at two years and ten months when he had only a few single words. The results from early hearing tests were inconclusive but later tests were satisfactory. His first assessment showed good symbolic play, good concept development and good visuo-motor skills. His attention control was well sustained, in an activity of his own choice, but he did not appreciate adult direction. Language comprehension showed a six month delay over his chronological age but with poor listening skills. Expression was limited to 5 – 10 single words with a limited consonant range and syllable structure. Therapy was offered and concentrated on expanding his listening skills, his expressive vocabulary and his range of consonants. He was referred to the nursery language unit at three years six months but was not thought mature enough to cope with the regime. He was 'a difficult child to control'. A year later, at the time of school entry, he was referred for a place in the primary language unit but had one term in mainstream school, with continued therapy support, until a place was available. A male cousin had attended the nursery language unit.

As primary language unit teacher I first met Mike in his Primary 1 classroom although his name had been known to me since his difficulties were first discussed at nursery stage. I spent a morning with him in his classroom, in a variety of situations, and below are my observations.

1. Mike was an attractive, well developed five year old who, although obviously well cared for, succeeded in looking totally dishevelled by the time he arrived at school.
2. He had a friendly, positive personality and a desperate desire to make friends and be liked by the other children. Despite these positive qualities, his behaviour was frequently impulsive and difficult to manage. His behavioural difficulties seemed largely due to a lack of self control rather than any desire to hurt anyone.
3. Mike appeared to have a high level of frustration due to his severe expressive problems and the resulting unintelligibility of his speech. Frustration did not prevent him trying to communicate and indeed, he talked a great deal, both loudly and at speed. Even at this early stage, it was apparent that his personality and sense of humour would prove to be great assets. (Mine were going to be greatly tested over the next year and a half!)
4. Despite being physically well co-ordinated he often seemed 'clumsy' and bumped into objects which were in his path. His general organisation seemed to be poor and his personal possessions were all over the place. His class operated an integrated day and Mike had obvious difficulty taking any responsibility for his own learning. Without the skills of his experienced teacher, he would have moved from one uncompleted task to another.
5. Although he had obvious areas of strength, he was making no progress in the early development of literacy skills.

We all felt that without the support of the language unit, Mike would become extremely vulnerable in an open plan school. Those who were on the receiving end of his boisterous and often aggressive behaviour would suffer too.

Criteria for admission

Admission procedures for the language units have now been standardised throughout the Region. I describe here the criteria and procedures operated in the unit at the time Mike was offered a place.

The initial assessment involved the speech and language therapist, teacher and educational psychologist with additional information from mainstream school and from the child's parents.

The unit provides places for seven children on a part-time basis, four afternoons a week. Following the initial assessment a decision was made based on the following criteria.

1. The child should be able to cope with the curricular demands of the mainstream school and with a shared placement.
2. The unit provides for children with specific speech and language disorders. There should be no predominant physical or sensory impairment, general developmental delay or behavioural disorder.
3. The composition of the group should be considered in relation to:
    a. the nature and severity of the delay/disorder;
    b. the balance between receptive and expressive problems.

Mike was admitted to the unit and after a brief settling in period, we began a multidisciplinary assessment of his needs followed by a joint planning of his programme.

My assessment took three forms:

1. close observation in a variety of contexts of his communication, social and motor skills;
2. assessment of his performance on a variety of tasks;
3. diagnostic assessment using the Aston Index.

Further to this assessment period the following picture of strengths and difficulties emerged.

Areas of strength

1. Mike showed a willingness to communicate and had good interactive skills despite his language difficulties.
2. He had a friendly outgoing personality and was responsive to praise and encouragement.
3. He demonstrated imaginative use of play and art and craft.
4. His visual perceptual skills were generally better than his auditory skills.
5. His gross motor skills were well developed.
6. He had adequate receptive language skills.
7. His family and school were concerned and supportive.

Areas of difficulty

1. Mike's attention control was very limited.
2. His auditory sequential memory was poor.
3. He had severe phonological problems.
4. He had problems in sound discrimination.
5. His fine motor control was poor in relation to drawing and writing.
6. There were problems in visual orientation and sequencing.
7. He had poor organisational ability in relation to his thoughts, language, work and possessions.
8. There was a general impulsivity and lack of control. All the above difficulties were seriously affecting Mike's development and progress in the areas of expressive language, literacy and social relationships.

Having a clear picture of Mike's strengths and weaknesses enabled us to have a greater understanding of the problems and frustrations with which he had to deal. In planning his programme it was important to make good use of his strengths while tackling his difficulties, maintain close contact with his family and with his school and liaise with family and school in a supportive way which did not place an additional burden on them.

On entry to the unit at five years one month his receptive language results were:

- Auditory Memory passed at the 3 year old level but failed at the 4 year old level.
- RLDS   Raw score 57   Age equiv. 4 years 8 months
- TROG   Raw score 8   Age equiv. 4 years 9 months
- BPVS   Raw score 43   Age equiv. 4 years 8 months
- EAT   Raw score 6   Age equiv. well below 3 years.

Expressive language, where intelligible, showed that syntax and morphology were considerably delayed. His sound inventory by this time had expanded to cover all stop sounds and fricatives but was limited to consonant-vowel-consonant and consonant-vowel-consonant-vowel structures. There was no vowel distortion. Although Mike successfully completed the tests for developmental articulatory dyspraxia there was some evidence of a motor problem. He found it difficult to sequence certain consonant vowel combinations. His gross motor skills were good but he did show some difficulty with fine motor skill activities. He could be very clumsy when undoing buttons, tying laces or in forming graphemes and found controlling his movements in small spaces very difficult. A detailed process analysis of his sound system showed:

velar fronting:	ta	–	car
stopping of fricatives	pu'	–	foot
	tummer	–	summer
	to'	–	shop
stopping of affricates	to'	–	chop
	dam	–	jam
liquid/glide simplification	we'	–	red
	we'er	–	letter

and in the structural processes initial and final cluster reduction:

poon	–	spoon
mas	–	mask

Mike also showed considerable difficulty in sequencing 'f' + vowel and 's' + vowel. This persisted when other processes were resolving.

Meeting Mike's needs

The general plan for the group and for each member's individual treatment was outlined at a meeting with the class teacher, the speech and language therapist and the education psychologist and the detailed activities were planned by the class teacher and speech and language therapist weekly. There was also a weekly perceptual motor programme (PMP) session with the PE specialist of which more later.

Auditory memory

Mike's auditory skills were tackled in three main areas:

1. listening games were incorporated into class activities;
2. listening to instructions and responding to them were an important part of PMP sessions and the resulting activity was one at which Mike could shine;
3. specific tape work 'Listen and Do', 'Listen and Colour', and the DLM auditory tape series. These last were at first closely supervised but gradually Mike worked through them on his own with less obvious supervision.

Vocabulary
Work on the understanding of spatial vocabulary was introduced in the PMP sessions where Mike jumped in and out, crawled under and jumped over, crawled through, ran between, stood beside, crept behind, crawled up, slid down, ran forwards, stepped backwards, stepped to the right side and then to the left. On his return to the classroom he drew a sequence of these activities and then described the drawings to the teacher who scribed for him. As will seem obvious, all the children benefited from these activities and they used this vocabulary much more quickly and freely than any of the previous language unit groups.

Work on enriching Mike's vocabulary was planned in conjunction with the mainstream school's class project. Where possible, extra time was spent ensuring that he understood and could use any new vocabulary.

Pronoun development
Initially this work began in individual therapy sessions but practice in usage was incorporated into class activities. As his sound system also matured Mike was able to use 'I', 'me', 'he', 'him', 'his', 'she', 'her', 'hers' appropriately. The plural forms developed very quickly after that.

Word order in sentences
Practice in using the correct word order when asking and answering questions was included in games and in the social activities of the class. Snack time, class outing and visits all provided the opportunity to use these new found skills in a natural situation.

Sound system

At the end of his first term in school Mike was showing little progress or interest in pre-reading activities. He had little awareness of the properties of sounds or an appreciation that these sounds could be represented on paper. There was concern that if this was not given consideration at this stage Mike could have considerable difficulties with reading. A two pronged attack was planned. Mike had to be given an awareness of sounds, where they were articulated, but also to be made aware of the similarities and differences between them and how he could use them to better effect. The Metaphon approach to phonological disorders would provide the answer to one aspect of the problem and an adaptation of the Sunnybank Colour Coding scheme the other.

The first process to be highlighted was velar fronting. Mike was able to produce the sounds in isolation but did not use them in spontaneous conversation. Work began on sharing some knowledge with Mike, that some sounds were made at the back of the mouth, some at the front; some were long sounds and some were short sounds. Mike already had the concept of back and front. At this stage therapy progressed quite quickly and he was using his new sounds in the session and in the classroom where he was more aware of his speech patterns. There was little carry over into everyday conversation where the need to do everything at great speed was more important to him. However, very gradually the velar sounds did appear in spontaneous speech. The stop sounds were now used freely and little work needed to be done to correct open syllabled speech which was very much in evidence in the early stages.

There was lots of discussion in the classroom about the properties of sounds and as the children learned to copy each new letter (using the approach in *The Foundations of Writing*) they were made aware of where it was produced – the grapheme was colour coded according to this place – and whether it was a long or a short sound. With Mike there had to be an intermediate stage. He was unable to make the straight phoneme-grapheme association and a pictorial representation of the sound was introduced, e.g. 'p' was a lip sound, was coloured red and was represented by a pipe. To be aware of what sound he had heard in a word Mike repeated it to himself, recognised it as a lip (red) sound, checked the chart to see the pipe and only then was he able to copy the 'p'. Only very gradually was he able to omit the pictorial stage – hear the phoneme and associate it with the grapheme.

Unstopping the fricatives, especially initial 'f' and 's' proved much more resistant to change. Mike seemed to have a particular problem in producing even a CV sequence and this persisted for a long time. He did however make headway with 'sh' and the affricates and initial 'f' and 's' were used spontaneously. Although he used these new skills in therapy sessions and when concentrating in the small group, Mike did not transfer these skills easily to everyday conversation. He was always in a hurry, always anxious to take an active part in any game which required physical activity. His lack of intelligible speech was never a hindrance to him when reacting with his peers. They had no problems in understanding him.

When Mike left the unit he still had not resolved final cluster reduction or liquid/glide simplification. At maximum concentration he could produce 'l' and 'l cluster' words correctly but there was no carry over. Nearly a year later he is still not consistent in these areas. His speech is intelligible – most of the time – but as the speed of utterance increases intelligibility decreases.

The classroom programme

In the programme which was planned for Mike were the following key elements, taking account of his identified strengths and difficulties.

Because Mike was an extremely active little boy – well co-ordinated and confident in the gym – it seemed sensible to use this strength as a vehicle for learning. A programme of learning through movement (Perceptual Motor Programme) was developed.

> A Perceptual Motor Programme is one which aims to teach the child perceptions and understandings of his/her world through movement/motor experiences.... It is not a motor programme but a perceptual motor programme where language is the key factor (Bulluss and Coles, 1987).

PMP activities took place both in the gym and in the classroom and involved joint planning between class teacher, speech and language therapist and PE specialist.

The main aims for Mike within the PMP programme were to:

1. improve and increase attention control;
2. extend skills in visual and auditory sequential memory;
3. improve ability in visual tracking;
4. reduce impulsivity and develop self control;
5. increase understanding and use of the language of position and space;
6. develop the ability to respond to and give instructions of increasing complexity.

Physical activity proved to be a very successful way of helping the children acquire and use the language of position, space and time. Activities were also planned which aimed to develop skills in tracking, orientation and sequencing, all of which are necessary in terms of reading and writing.

PMP activities involved:

- listening to an instruction;
- absorbing the instruction;
- repeating the instruction;
- processing and acting upon the instruction;
- giving an instruction to someone else.

Large format letter and word cards were used in the classroom and in the gym and active games were planned which aimed to develop word recognition as well as tracking and sequencing skills. The Sunnybank Programme was used to help develop phonological awareness and phoneme/grapheme correspondence through use of *The Foundations of Writing* letter formation. The material and rationale within *The Foundations of Writing* linked extremely well with the Perceptual Motor Programme and was also a resource used in Mike's base school. PMP sessions were always followed by a drawing/modelling activity related to the session. Mike used his drawing or model as a visual prompt to help sequence his story. It is important to note that when 'scribing' his story, I always used correct structures to provide him with a good linguistic model. The correct form was written down. *The Foundations of Writing* was also used to improve fine motor skills, aid sequential storytelling and increase descriptive vocabulary.

As well as using the PMP and *The Foundations of Writing*, Mike's auditory and visual perceptual skills were enhanced through a planned listening skills programme and through use of the BBC computer. When giving instructions in a functional context we insisted on Mike giving and sustaining eye contact, and remaining in one place for the duration of the instruction. Gaining his attention was not always easy but was essential to his progress. His parents also began to insist on this level of attention control.

Because his comprehension was fairly good, we developed a programme of listening activities using commercially produced material and a listening centre with individual headphones. Initially he worked in a small group with adult supervision. The aim was that eventually he would work independently on a short activity.

BBC computer programmes were used to improve turn taking and concentration, directionality and orientation, and hand/eye coordination. Mike really enjoyed computer activities so they were also used as reward (or bribery!).

No formal reading scheme was used initially as Mike lacked the basic pre-requisites and consequently had past experiences of failure. He was later introduced to Crown Readers and with use of games, activities and much reinforcement in the unit and from the learning support teacher in his base school, he began to make progress.

Mike was formally reviewed one year after admission. Although he was beginning to make significant progress, it was agreed by everyone present, that he should return for a further term, on two afternoons a week, to consolidate and build on this. Almost one year after returning full time to his own school, Mike is sustaining progress. There has been considerable improvement in his concentration and application to tasks, fine motor control, intelligibility, behaviour and reading. His phonic skills are developing and phoneme/grapheme correspondence is complete. His auditory memory remains poor but his listening skills are considerably better in a small group situation. Although he still has considerable difficulties with spelling he is eager to overcome these. He continues to have learning support and speech therapy.

References

Bulluss, J. and Coles, P. (1987) *Perceptual Motor Programmes*. Victoria, Australia, PJ Developments

Jackson, W. and Michael, B. (1986) *The Foundations of Writing: A Report of the Project*. Edinburgh, Consultative Committee on the Curriculum

A PAL for Children with Learning Difficulties

Lynda Booth and Peter Gregor

Introduction

PAL – Predictive Adaptive Lexicon – is a predictive text entry program which has been developed at the University of Dundee MicroCentre (Swiffin et al., 1987; 1988). Now a commercially available product, PAL runs on any IBM compatible computers, usually in connection with a word processor. The program exploits the redundancy in natural language to reduce the number of key presses needed to type a piece of text. While the user is typing, a short menu of word predictions appears near to the cursor and one of these predictions may be selected using an appropriate key press. PALSTAR, a word processor with simple commands and the capability to display large print was designed and developed for use in schools and in conjunction with PAL. Figure 10.1 shows an example of the screen layout of PALSTAR with PAL's predictive window superimposed on it.

Fig. 10.1: PAL being used with the PALSTAR word processor

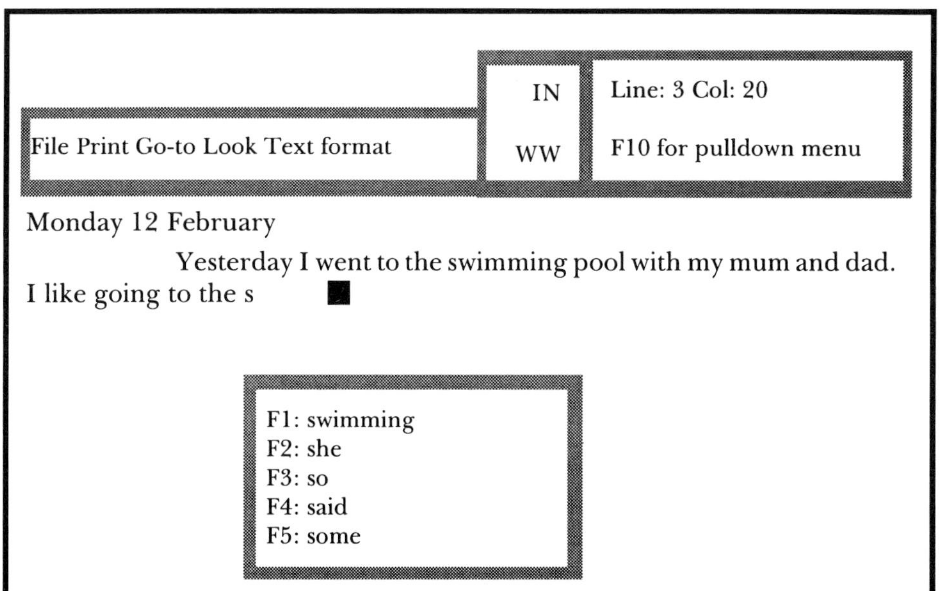

This chapter is substantially based upon an article that appeared in *Child Language Teaching and Therapy* (1992) **8 (2)**, and has been reproduced by permission of Edward Arnold (Publishers) Ltd.

When a prediction is selected, by pressing the appropriate function key, the word is completed by PAL as though it had been typed in full. If the prediction list does not contain the word the user is trying to type, she/he enters another character and PAL will produce a new list on the basis of the characters entered so far. This process continues until either a prediction is selected or a word is typed fully and terminated with a space or punctuation symbol. PAL attempts to offer the most recently, frequently used words by offering predictions from a dictionary of words which contains statistical information relating to frequency and recency. If the desired word is not in the dictionary it has to be entered in full, but PAL automatically acquires such words, adds them to the dictionary, and thereafter offers them as predictions.

To make the system as versatile and useful as possible PAL also has a number of other special features, such as turning off the auto-repeat on the keyboard. There is an optional 'key beep' to give positive feedback, and the shift and control keys can be latched to assist users who cannot hold down two keys simultaneously. A version of PAL is available which displays a standard scanned matrix as well as the word predictions in the window. This is shown in Figure 10.2. A single or double switch can then be used to control the scanned matrix. These switches may be operated by the arm, head, a mouth tube or whatever method is most

Fig. 10.2: Scanning PAL being used with the PALSTAR word processor

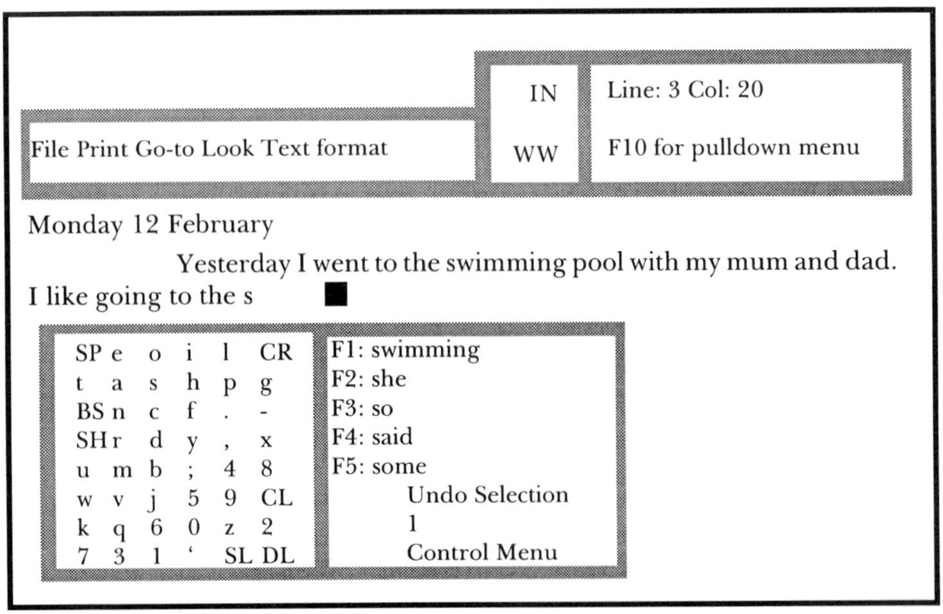

appropriate to the user (Brophy et al., 1989). The particular design of PAL has produced a predictive text entry system which has proved to be very successful for a wide range of users (Newell et al., 1991).

Introducing PAL into schools

In collaboration with the local education authority, a major program was begun to introduce PAL to children in a special educational setting (Beattie et al., 1990; Booth et al., 1990). A booklet describing how to use PAL and PALSTAR was produced with the aim of enabling teachers who were unfamiliar with computers to train by themselves at home or school. It was also decided to encourage teachers to use PAL and PALSTAR themselves to produce pupil reports and copies of their forward planning programmes. In this way teachers would become familiar with the programs and be confident in assisting the children on the research project. Initially the programs were taken to the schools and demonstrated to head teachers, teachers and carers involved with the children.

It had been intended to focus the work on children with physical disability. Many of the children within the schools, however, presented with classic learning difficulties, as well as physical disability. It was observed that, after using PAL for two to three weeks, the children became aware that prediction could assist their own spelling problems and they looked at the predictions for assistance. Even children with severe spelling difficulties were very often able to produce the first letters of words although they could not spell the word correctly in full. They were also able to recognise words presented visually within the prediction list even when the list was composed of a number of similar looking words. The research plan was thus revised to include children with spelling and/or language dysfunction.

Research study

The primary aim of the research study was to examine the functional use of PAL within a normal educational environment with pupils with a wide variety of special educational needs. It was conducted within local schools by a special education teacher who had been seconded to the project from the local education authority. The study was done with substantial assistance from the classroom teachers and care assistants. The major results of this study were in the form of comments and opinions from the class teachers, together with the observations of the research teacher. These were supported by the results from some experimental probes which were applied by the research teacher at intervals during the study. The type of probe used depended on the individual circumstances of the pupils.

The study was divided into two phases, each of between six and nine months duration, with nine and eight children in the two phases respectively. When the availability of the equipment allowed, the teachers used PAL with other children in the class. In total, approximately fifty children with a wide range of educational needs were exposed to the software within an eighteen month period.

PAL was introduced to each child in the study individually. Following an initial assessment of the needs and capabilities of the child, a work programme was devised for each of them. The particular way PAL was to be used, the curriculum within which it would operate, and the methods of assessment of its contribution to the child's education depended on the individual child and the way he or she responded to using PAL. Detailed note books were kept by the teachers during the project. These included copies of all the work done by the child using PAL, annotated to indicate the conditions under which it had been produced, plus general comments on how the child was responding to the work he or she was being asked to do.

At the end of a period of approximately six months, teachers or therapists were asked to complete an individual questionnaire for each child on the value of PAL in the classroom. Information from the teachers' note books and data collected from the research teacher during her weekly visits to the schools were collated to produce individual case-studies of each child. (See Figure 10.3.)

The use of PAL in the classroom

The pupils in the study were introduced to the programs in an initial training period of roughly one hour per week for four to six weeks. During these training sessions, teachers were consulted as to how the program could be introduced and used within the classroom. Teacher support was a vital element in this study and the co-operation and interest shown by the staff led to excellent relations between school and the university.

It was found that most of the children required only a limited amount of keyboard training, and soon became familiar with the program. Following the training period of four one-hour sessions, the pupils were left with the computers to use them whenever it was appropriate within the normal school timetable. Subsequently schools were visited weekly by the research teacher to provide support and suggestions to the classroom teacher, and also to assess and evaluate the progress of the children.

The children in the primary schools used the program for all written English work. The secondary pupils began by using it in one subject, usually English, then extended its use to other subjects where writing was a problem. The software was used in a range of subjects which included Social Studies, Biology, Home Economics, Craft and Design, Technical, Business Studies, Office Management, History and Music. The computer was taken home by the secondary pupils, to allow them to carry out their homework, and to extend their school work at home. Learning support teachers involved with the children were also able to use the computer in their resource bases.

Fig. 10.3: Profile of children in the case-studies

Client	Age	Comments	Ability to use a keyboard	Presenting problems
(1)AA	18	Cerebral-palsied Wheelchair user Severely dysarthric	uses keyguard	physical
(2)CK	9	Cerebral-palsied Wheelchair user Severely athetoid Moderate dysarthria	uses keyguard	physical
(3)PM	10	Muscular dystrophy	fair to poor (used mouse)	physical
(4) JA	14	Specific learning difficulties	good	spelling
(5)IM	11	Muscular dystrophy	fair	physical and spelling
(6)CW	14	Cerebral-palsied Specific learning difficulties Visual impairment	good (one hand)	physical and spelling
(7)MT	12	Cerebral-palsied Wheelchair user Non-speaking	uses keyguard	physical and spelling
(8)IC	10	Severe developmental delay	good	language
(9)RC	10	Dyspraxic Telegrammatic speech and writing	good	language
(10)BI	14	Down's syndrome	fair	language
(11)BC	16	Cerebral-palsied Mild dysarthria Hearing loss	good	physical and language
(12)AM	19	Cerebral-palsied Non-speaking	moderate	physical and language
(13)KM	15	Fragile X Poor speech	fair	physical and language
(14)DS	9	Cerebral-palsied Non-speaking	uses keyguard	physical and language
(15)DL	8	Cerebral-palsied	moderate	physical and language
(16)CH	10	Lowe's syndrome Visual impairment	good	reluctant writer
(17)BN	11	Spelling disorder	good	reluctant writer

Results

A summary of the major findings in this study is given below, followed by illustrative case-studies.

Questionnaire responses

Each child's teacher or therapist was asked to rate the contribution PAL had made to aspects of their pupil's work on a scale of 1 to 5, as follows:

1. a great improvement;
2. a significant improvement;
3. some improvement;
4. little improvement;
5. no improvement.

The areas which were rated are shown in the following list:

Indep.	Creation of independence and development of confidence
Motiv.	Motivation to work
Vocab.	Increase in vocabulary
Lang.	Stimulation of language
Conc.	Increase in concentration span
Teacher Time	Reduction in teacher time
Present.	Competence in presentation and basic literacy
Phy.M	Reduced physical movement
Speed	Increased speed of completing work
Spell.	Accuracy of spelling
Learn.	Improved learning.

In certain cases, the pupils themselves also filled in a questionnaire. Results show that teachers and pupils saw improvements in all aspects of work, the particular improvements highlighted by them depending on the characteristics of each child.

A summary of the results of the forced choice section of the questionnaire responses is shown in Figure 10.4. The overall response of all the teachers to PAL was very positive. The rating scales showed significant improvement in independence and confidence, motivation, stimulation of language, speed of completing work and learning (these results were significant at either the 1% or 5% level).

Some increase was reported in vocabulary size, concentration span, presentation and basic literacy, and accuracy of spelling, and a reduction was reported in teacher time, and physical movement. The variety of children within the study, however, should be borne in mind in any interpretation of these averaged results.

Speed of composition and time to complete tasks

In the case of children with severe physical disabilities, PAL was found to reduce the time taken to produce work. The key savings produced by PAL (see Swiffin et al., 1987) also meant that writing with PAL was less fatiguing, and both these factors encouraged physically disabled children to produce more written work. The results from these speed tests, which are supported by teacher's opinions (see Figure 10.4), however, are meant only to give a guide to what can be achieved using a predictive system. Formal speed tests, particularly with children, can give very variable results: these are dependent on a wide range of parameters including

Fig. 10.4: Results from PAL questionnaire[a]

Improvement	1 Great	2 Significant	3 Some	4 Litle	5 No
Independence and confidence	7	6	4	0	0*
Motivation to work	3	12	1	0	1**
Increase vocabulary	3	7	5	1	1
Stimulate language (16 children only)	2	9	5	0	0**
Increase concen-tration span	3	3	7	2	0
Reduce teacher time (15 children ony)	3	3	7	2	0
Presentation and basic literacy	6	6	3	2	0
Reduce physical movement (12 children only)	5	4	3	0	0
Increased speed of completing work	8	5	3	0	1**
Accuracy of spelling	5	6	4	1	1
Learning	3	6	8	0	0**

a Results are shown as scores out of 17, except in those cases where the questions were not applicable to all the children.

* Significant at the 5% level

** Significant at the 1% level

the particular vocabulary within the system, its relationship to the text being created, and also the style of this text. The speed with which a physically disabled person can construct text is even more variable, as it will also depend upon other variables such as their motivation and physical condition at the time of the test.

PAL dictionaries

PAL is normally introduced to a new user with one of two standard dictionaries. These have 1000 and 5000 words respectively. Most of the children were given the 1000 word dictionary but two pupils were given a 5000 word dictionary. Some children were initially provided with small specialised dictionaries which, in one case, consisted of only ten words.

PAL is adaptive and thus, even if it is supplied with a standard dictionary, it can automatically capture each user's personal vocabulary and add it to its dictionary. This significantly increases the probability of the correct word being predicted. During this study, every child had his/her own dictionary, which grew in size and in appropriateness as personal words, and words related to the subjects being studied, were automatically added. The recency factor in PAL's design ensures that new words are predicted before other words in the dictionary which may have been used more often, but less recently. The effect of this was to reinforce the use of new words and this was felt to be a significant factor in the acceptance of the program by teachers and children within an educational environment.

Use of dictionaries

The size of the PAL dictionary gives some indication of how the system is adapting to the individual needs of the child and the curriculum. In general, the most rapid increase in dictionary size occurs in the early stages of use of the system, but new topics introduced into the curriculum produce sudden further increases in dictionary size. The two children, who started with a 5000 word dictionary, found that most of the words they required were already in the dictionary. Nevertheless, during the period of the study, they both added over 100 new words to the system. (In its current implementation the maximum dictionary size for PAL is 6800 words – with an adaptive system, a dictionary size significantly above this figure is unlikely to provide much advantage). For the child with a severe developmental delay, although the rate of increase in words used was not dramatic, a steady progress occurred throughout the study.

The facility to add to dictionaries as an activity in its own right was reported to be very useful in an educational environment, with teachers and pupils adding new vocabulary as the child progressed. This would be done by the teacher or pupil keying in vocabulary from a reading scheme, or a new topic before it was introduced to the curriculum. Many of the children also realised the importance of their own vocabulary being in the dictionary and many of them added new vocabulary in connection with a particular theme or topic which was to be introduced to the class in the near future. The teacher provided the books or lists with the new vocabulary and the child was allowed to select words and add them to the dictionary. This activity was completely new for these children and gave them an added interest and confidence in coping with the written word.

PAL is a word-based system, but it does include a facility which allows phrases of up to twenty characters to be inserted into the dictionary and be treated and presented as a single prediction. For some of the children, this was used to great advantage by storing the child's full name, address, or school plus a few other groups of words which the child normally used together. This was found to be very motivating particularly with those children with poor language skills and/or physical disabilities.

Although it is possible for a child to use PAL with different dictionaries for different subjects, this particular facility was not used within the case-studies presented here. Multiple dictionaries may be particularly helpful in the secondary school setting where vocabulary for individual subjects can be very specialised. It also could be effective when a new reading scheme is introduced to a child. (In this case, immediately prior to introducing the scheme, the teacher could provide the child with a special PAL dictionary containing all the words in that reading scheme.)

Effects on spelling ability

With the majority of the children in the study, teachers reported that the use of PAL within the normal curriculum was reducing the spelling errors in their work substantially. In order to obtain a numerical assessment of these effects, six of the children were dictated passages which they had to type both with and without PAL. To provide a better comparison, the passage dictated to a particular child was identical in both situations, but writing with prediction always preceded writing without prediction as, if there was any order effect, this would bias the results against prediction. Over all the children, the words which were incorrectly spelled reduced when they were assisted by PAL by 70%.

The improved spelling and the quality of the written work which the children could produce was a major reason for their improved motivation.

Unaided spelling

Although the standard Burt and Aston tests showed little or no improvement in spelling age during the course of this study, it is interesting to compare words children had difficulties with at the beginning of the project with their attempts at these same words at the end of the project. Some of the children were tested with a list of approximately twenty words taken from their school work at the beginning of the trial period and were re-tested at the end. The attempts at many words which they were still not able to spell correctly, were closer to the correct spelling than was the case at the beginning of the trial. This improvement could change a completely indecipherable word to one which, although not correct, could be easily understood in context.

PAL and language skills

In essence PAL simply offers word predictions to users and thus provides key saving and assistance with the spelling of words. In use, however, PAL was found to increase the opportunities for the children with very limited language skills to develop their written language and gave them a sense of achievement and increased confidence. This produced some improvements in language skills. In the case of the Bliss users, PAL improved the ability to produce either correctly spelt words or good approximations to the correct spelling. For some children, this highlighted problems with word order and other language skills on which the teachers could then concentrate.

Vocalisation when using PAL

One interesting occurrence was that, while using PAL, most of the speaking children vocalised as they wrote, articulating clearly and breaking down the words into syllabic units. This vocalisation helped stress the initial letter of a word which the child wanted to find in prediction. When working with children with severe language disorder, it can be helpful to encourage them to articulate written words in order to assist the establishment of an association between speech and symbols. It was observed that children using PAL tended to do this without having to be prompted and reminded, and a speech therapist commented that this should help them in the process of developing speech and language (Brophy, 1989).

Reluctant writers

The effects of the program on children who were reluctant to write was very dramatic. PAL was found to be particularly relevant for those children with special educational needs who had encountered difficulties for some considerable time with accompanying feelings of failure and frustration. The introduction of PAL often produced a happier and more relaxed atmosphere resulting in emotional as well as academic progress being made. An extremely tense fifteen year old boy with a severe spelling disorder was observed to relax when using PAL and showed no signs of his usual anxiety when being asked to produce written work. Various subject teachers commented on his change in attitude. In this and other children's cases, it was also reported that the use of PAL helped to bridge the gap between home and school. Some parents who had not previously made contact with the school now became more involved. The program gave satisfaction and motivation to both parents and the child who was often experiencing a measure of success for the first time. This helped the school establish links with parents.

Case-study 1

JA is an articulate fifteen year old, with a specific learning difficulty, in a mainstream secondary school.

- Reading Age: 7:2
- Spelling Age: 6:1
- Keyboarding Skills: good

Special educational needs

Reading and writing had been a major problem for JA since the infant class in primary school. Learning support and class teachers had acted as scribes for all tests and written work. Teachers were urged to use simple vocabulary whenever possible. JA could barely cope with words of four or five letters, not even being able to spell his own name. The boy's severe spelling disorder had been a problem throughout his school career, making him frustrated and apprehensive when carrying out writing tasks. He never voluntarily carried out school work in his own time.

Introduction and use of PAL in the classroom

JA was given a 1000 word dictionary to which had been added his name and address and other words which were important to him. PAL thus enabled JA to type his name and address correctly and write about his personal interests, neither of which had he been able to do. He developed enthusiasm, confidence and a self-esteem his teachers had never seen before. He had a more positive attitude towards his work, coming into school half an hour earlier in the morning to enable him to print out homework completed the evening before. Lunch times found him in the resource base finishing written work from various subjects. Subject teachers commented on the change in the boy's personality and attitude to work. Parents, who previously were not involved with the school, now made contact and made enquires about the program.

There was not a great deal of improvement in JA's unaided spelling and it is felt that he has such a severe spelling disorder that he will always need to rely on a program such as PAL to give him the confidence and support necessary for producing written work.

Examples of work

Written composition without prediction:

olrh hom farm

my farm is arbo it is ol plelbo and can be yoot for seros it as a qora duon ner the bottom I get chat and go duon to the qora and see jack

Written from dictation using prediction:

Orchil home farm

my farm is arbo it is ploughable and can be ytt for sero it at a quarry down need the bottom I get changed and go down to the quarry and see jack

Questionnaire results (teacher)
Indep. 1 Motiv. 2 Vocab. 2 Lang. 1 Conc. 1 Teacher Time 3 Present. 1 Phy.M. 2 Speed 3 Spell. 3 Learn. 3

Questionnaire results (pupil)
Indep. 3 Motiv. 4 Vocab. 3 Lang. 4 Conc. 3 Teacher Time 3 Present. 3 Phy.M. 4 Speed 1 Spell. 3 Learn. 4

Comments from questionnaire

- He was prepared to 'have a go' at written work that he had never offered before. Self-esteem and confidence were low but, once he had the working knowledge of the computer, he very obviously 'grew' particularly with peers. *[teacher]*
- I write better with it – spelling. Easier to read my work. *[JA]*
- He had no motivation to work and this attitude goes back as far as Primary 2 in records. *[teacher]*
- I hate most schoolwork. *[JA]*
- He leads a very isolated life outside school and was a 'loner' in school. Confidence gained over the last six months has allowed him to attempt new words, written and oral. *[teacher]*
- It shows you the correct spelling and I use more words because of this.' *[JA]*
- Delaying tactics he used previously disappeared completely. *[teacher]*
- You can do more in a shorter time than if you're writing. *[JA]*
- This research has been so successful in every way that I would like the pupil to continue. I fear that he might just revert to being an isolate and 'switching off' in school work. Psychologically it seems cruel to withdraw a resource that offered positive help or, as he said himself 'it was too good to last'. [Fortunately it proved possible for the Education Authority to provide replacement equipment.]

Case-study 2

RC is a ten year old boy who attends a mainstream primary school and has only recently had a one-to-one teacher to assist his special needs.

- Reading Age: 7:5
- Spelling Age: 7:4
- Keyboarding Skills: good

Special educational needs

RC has a severe language disorder and a history of communication difficulties. The problems of language and written work had increased as he progressed through the school. RC's speech was immature, lacked rhythm and intonation and he used key words and telegraphic forms to convey meaning. He has great difficulty formulating sentences. His speech problem does not inhibit him and he chats freely to children, staff and visitors to the school. His writing reflected his telegramatic speech and he tended to use familiar simple words that he could spell. His teacher reported that his sight vocabulary was quite large, but his ability to recall the words when writing was poor. RC tended to be easily distracted and lost interest in any language work in a very short period of time. When asked to spell words he would often say, 'I can't spell that', and make no attempt to do so. He demonstrated the truth of the statement as, when coaxed to attempt those words, it was always found that he could not spell them and was very aware of his failures.

PAL was introduced with 1000 word dictionary plus some personal words. RC quickly realised the importance of having his own words in the dictionary and the assistance he was given by the words in prediction. His problems were so great and his self-esteem so poor that, after only one training session, it was decided to leave the computer and program permanently in the classroom for RC's use. He could recognise words with which he had always had spelling problems when they were predicted, and he began to take great advantage of the help provided by the predictions. RC quickly became the expert in the classroom, the teacher/pupil role being reversed for the first time. His teacher sought his advice, confessing that she was not too familiar with computers and looked to him for help and support. She employed another strategy, which boosted RC's confidence, of asking him to demonstrate the program to another pupil who had a spelling disorder. The words used by the other pupil were automatically added to RC's dictionary and, if they were writing a story, they were able to discuss what they were going to write and RC was able to produce a piece of text using vocabulary suggested by his friend.

This child's spelling did not improve on formal tests, but he was able to spell familiar words more accurately at the end of the case-study than he had been at the beginning. Improvements in unaided spelling continued beyond the end of the formal study. At a later date, an early piece of writing from the study was dictated again to him, after a gap of fourteen months. The improvement in spelling in this passage is shown below.

Examples of free writing
9/2/89 Dictation with prediction:

> *I have 2 sisters and no brithers My mum works up bark sreet sroing crochns and preios. My dad works mraxch new merchs. I play criet and sroer I woch tv I like lost in srare I like nreamper work*

21/4/89 Free writing with prediction:

> *On monday I have rice krispies at brikvest time is seven o'colock at morning atter real to school I but in pleat with mild and sooker in set room.*

24/4/91 Dictation of (9/2/89) passage without prediction, showing improvement in spelling:

> *i have two sister and no brothers my mum works in bank streetsawing cousing and pilos. My dad works at maxtrex new mecheans. i play cricket and snooker. i watch televisin i like lost in space i like nunber work.*

Questionnaire results
Indep. 2 Motiv. 2 Vocab. 3 Lang. 2 Conc. 2 Teacher Time 3 Present. 3 Phy.M. n/a Speed 3 Spell. 1 Learn. 2

Comments from questionnaire
- Produces free writing with more confidence. Before PAL, he was very reluctant to write. *[teacher]*
- Vocabulary is still very basic. He has a poor understanding of language but is happy to scan the vocabulary [predicted by PAL] and comments on words he has inserted for reading or project activities. *[teacher]*
- He works for much longer periods of time. *[teacher]*
- He realises he can tackle new or hitherto untried words with the help of PAL and so is stimulated into writing more. *[teacher]*
- Word recognition is very good and continuous use of PAL has consolidated many words which he cannot sound out. *[teacher]*

Conclusions

PAL, a predictive writing system, has been found to help children with a range of special needs and was flexible enough to adapt as children develop and progress through using the program. PAL has assisted children with physical disabilities by reducing keystrokes. This allowed them to produce written work much faster and with much less effort. Children with spelling problems have used the predictions to great effect. The quality of written work of poor spellers improved significantly. With the younger children, there was some evidence of improvements in unaided written work during the course of the project. PAL also increased the opportunities for children with limited language skills by developing their written language, increasing their confidence and giving them a sense of achievement. It allowed children to concentrate on the content of their writing rather than the process of letter formation and spelling. The amount of written work children have been prepared to produce has increased, and in some cases more than doubled. Even in the case of a child with a severe developmental delay PAL was found to produce a substantial improvement in written work.

Teachers also commented on an increase in the written vocabulary that the children were prepared to use. In addition, the improvement in motivation, confidence, self-esteem and a degree of success never before experienced were observed. These led to the children developing new positive attitudes towards attaining literacy.

The research study has shown that a predictive writing system, such as PAL, is able to help a child with a range of special needs and is flexible enough to adapt as the child develops and progresses through using the program. PAL has been found particularly valuable for assisting in the integration of children with special needs into mainstream schools. It gave integrated children a greater access to the curriculum and provided opportunities in education which had been denied to them due to their disabilities.

A spelling corrector program has been developed which is compatible with PAL as a further assistance for children with very severe spelling problems and research and development of the PAL program is being extended to investigate how syntax and semantics can help produce more accurate predictions. In this way, it is hoped, the assistance this predictive word processor can provide to people with various categories of language dysfunction will be extended.

Acknowledgements

The work reported here was supported by The Department of Trade and Industry (UK), The Scottish Education Department, The Training Agency (UK), Tayside Regional Council, and the University of Dundee.

The authors wish to acknowledge help from other staff in the MicroCentre at Dundee University, substantial assistance received from Miss K. Treacy (Assistant Director, Special Education, Tayside Region), many teachers working in schools in Tayside Region, and their debt of gratitude to the children who took part in the case-studies reported.

References

Beattie, W., Booth, L., Newell, A. F. and Arnott, J. L. (1990) The role of predictive computer programs in special education. *Augmentative and Alternative Communication,* **6 (2)**, 89

Booth, L., Beattie, W. and Newell, A. F. (1990) I know what you mean. *Special Children,* **41**, 26-27

Brophy, B., Colvin, J. B., Fuller, D., Swiffin, A. L., Newell, A. F., Condie, D. N. and Hood, H. E. (1989) Communication aids for the neurologically impaired child and young adult in the school and community. *Final Report to the Scottish Home and Health Department*

Newell, A. F., Arnott, J. L., Booth L., Beattie, W., and Brophy, B. (1991) The use of the PAL word prediction system to improve literacy. Submitted for publication to *Augmentative and Alternative Communication*

Swiffin, A. L., Arnott, J. L., and Newell, A. F. (1987) Adaptive and predictive techniques in a communication prosthesis. *Augmentative and Alternative Communication,* **3**, 181-191

Swiffin A. L., Arnott, J. L., and Brophy, B., (1988) Function and content words in a predictive system. *Proceedings of the International Conference of the Association for the Advancement of Rehabilitation Engineering,* Montreal, Canada

Note

PAL and PALSTAR are trade marks of the predictive text entry system and an associated word processor marketed by Lander Software Ltd, 74 Victoria Crescent Road, Glasgow G12 9JN.

Parental Involvement and Peer Tutoring in Oracy

Keith Topping

Oracy – to spoken language what literacy is to written language. Not a pretty word, to be sure, and you may prefer simply 'speaking and listening', or (more jargonistically) 'expressive and receptive language'.

In this paper the development of interest in oracy and in parents and peers as tutors will be briefly described, before considering some relevant research evidence. Issues in the organisation of parent and peer tutoring in oracy will then be summarised, prior to reviewing a range of resources and materials suitable for the purpose.

Current context

Recent years have seen greater emphasis on oral work in schools, coupled with trends towards more co-operative group work and continuous assessment of progress. Language is seen increasingly as more than a way of communicating ideas, transmitting information and checking understanding. Not merely thought in transit, language is itself a form of thought, the use of which can sharpen, reformulate or transform inner hidden ideas.

As interest in oracy has grown, a number of oracy projects have been launched. The Assessment of Performance Unit mounted a Language Monitoring Project on oracy assessment. The National Oracy Project took off, and individual LEAs have launched their own local initiatives (e.g. the ILEA Oracy Project, the Bury Oracy Project, the Shropshire Oracy Project and the Wiltshire Oracy Project). However, many of these were purely focused on oracy in the classroom, and although many involved co-operative peer group work in that setting, few explored the potential of parental involvement.

To talk of 'parental involvement and peer tutoring in oracy' is really a bit of a nonsense. Parents have always been by far the most important teachers of oracy to their preschool children. Much vocabulary is subsequently picked up from the peer group or siblings. The media of television, radio and books have a substantial effect. Teachers probably come in fourth in terms of influence.

For the busy teacher overwhelmed by the demands of the National or 5–14 Curriculum, fitting in specific time for oracy development can be very difficult. Some teachers assert hopefully that oracy development is occurring across the curriculum 'all the time', just like literacy development. Whether this is actually happening in reality is quite another question. Certainly the class teacher will never have time to give all members of the class sufficient individual attention to directly affect their oracy skills.

In this situation, the role of the teacher must become that of an organiser of effective learning, designing and monitoring interactive experiences and skills practice, flexibly attuned to the needs of individuals. This is particularly necessary for children with special needs in the language area – better staffing ratios have the inherent risk of creating increased dependence on the teacher.

Special needs children often have difficulty in retaining new skills and generalising them to situations outside the classroom and outside the school. This is another very important reason why teachers need to spend a portion of their precious time on organising parental involvement. Through good management by teachers and other professionals, the profound impact of the major influences on oracy development (parents and peers) can be heightened.

Parents who are given extra support and training have been demonstrated to accelerate the development of oracy skills in a variety of different projects: compensatory or Headstart projects, programmes for children with specific language dysfunction, and schemes for children with language deficits associated with global developmental delay and/or autism (see Chapter 9 in Topping 1986 for a summary of the research evidence).

There is relatively little in the literature on peer tutoring in oracy, the more usual emphasis tending to be on co-operative group work in this curricular area. However, there are reports on peer tutoring in the learning of sign language, in the learning of foreign languages at secondary level and in learning English as a second language (see Chapter 6 in Topping 1988 for a summary of the research evidence).

Peer tutoring with children with specific language difficulties was reported as early as 1971 by Bailey et al., who modified the articulation errors of two boys aged twelve and thirteen years by systematic programming of their peers. Although the literature on peer tutoring with such children is generally sparse, this does not of course mean that such tutoring is not happening.

Studies of parental involvement in oracy development with children with specific language difficulties are worth considering in more detail.

Research on parental involvement

A case-study of a non-speaking child of three years six months was described by Whitehurst et al. (1972). The level of parent-initiated conversation and level and use of initiative prompts were systematically varied. Results showed that when either behaviour was present at a high level, the child's use of language accelerated;

when both were used simultaneously, the child's language accelerated most of all. Just asking the child questions appeared to have negligible stimulatory impact.

Four mothers of children with a variety of communication disorders received training in behaviour change techniques at a two-day workshop reported by Carpenter and Augustine (1973). The mothers were selected for motivation and ability to benefit from such training. Written and verbal instruction, video-tape observation and analysis, role-play, modelling, practice, video and verbal feedback and group discussion were included. Home lesson plans were prepared by the professionals, with specific objectives and criteria for each day written out, together with appropriate parental responses and a chart for recording. When children reached a criterion of 80% correct performance on two consecutive days, the next lesson was supplied. Overall, three of the four parents proved able to modify their children's communicative behaviour over the period in question.

Miller and Sloane (1976) trained five parents of non-verbal children to modify antecedents to and consequences of their children's vocalisations. Parent training was in homes, by verbal instruction, live modelling with their child, feedback, reinforcement and self-recording. Content revolved round parental modelling of sounds, prompting and positive and negative reinforcement for accurate imitation or vocalisation on the child's part. Parents rapidly learned to carry this out effectively and improvements in child vocalisations generalised to other times and settings in the home.

The question of generalisation of parent training was also addressed by Mulac and Tomlinson (1977). Nine children aged between four and six years were assigned to one of three conditions: (a) a programme with large home component, (b) a programme with small home component, and (c) a control programme. Group (a) received eight sessions, conducted in the family home and out 'on location', during which the professional modelled the required procedures with the child and then monitored parental practice. All the children were post-tested on the trained tasks. On the tasks assessed in the centre, all members of groups (a) and (b) had a pre-test score of 0% and a post-test score of 100%. However, performance on the same tasks in the home setting was quite different, with the extended home programme group (a) doing significantly better than the predominantly centre-based programme group (b). Neither group (b) nor group (c) showed significant out-of-centre improvement.

A more naturalistic study was conducted by Stevenson et al. (1982). Twenty-two children aged two years six months to three years six months, of below average socio-economic status and without hearing loss but with substantive expressive language delay, were allocated to matched experimental and control groups. The experimental families were subsequently visited at home by a speech therapist approximately twenty-two times over a six month period. Programme content was individualised, the therapist working with the child in the mother's presence and lending toys and books for use between visits. Significant pre-test to post-test differences were found on the Reynell Scale, but both the experimental and control group made gains.

Training workshops on the development of 'motherese' to facilitate the progress of forty children from two to five years of age with expressive language delay were evaluated by Weistuch and Brown (1987). Mean length of utterance and use of multi-word utterances increased significantly in the experimental group.

Howlin (1984) provided a review of the relevant literature, in which she considered the language environment of normal children (and the effect of parental speech) as compared with that of linguistically handicapped children. Her review of the involvement of parents in language 'therapy' covered techniques used, type of child involved, levels of parental involvement, evaluation research designs, different treatment effects, and the influence of parental competence. It was noted that behavioural programmes were the most popular, if frequency of appearance in the literature was anything to go by.

A further review of 'training parents to be language facilitators' emanated from McDade and Varnedoe (1987). Parent training content included teaching interactive styles (e.g. establishing semantic contingency, eliciting appropriate language) and learning facilitative techniques (e.g. positive feedback, expansions, use of comments). Variation in the process and effectiveness of parent training are described.

Clearly, in some of these studies input to parents has involved a level of resourcing beyond the scope of most schools. However, parent involvement programmes do not need to be so complex nor so expensive in teacher time to be effective, as a study by Swinson and Ellis (1988) shows. These workers encouraged and supported the parents of children aged three years and over to simply read them stories on a regular basis. The result was child gains on tests of language skills and improved listening in the classroom.

However, successful parent or peer tutoring on even the smallest scale requires careful organisation.

Organisation

Some of the studies in the literature have clearly taken a highly structured approach to parent training, so the 'parent curriculum' is very weighty and the transmitted techniques vastly complex and laden with jargon. Obviously, such an approach will not reach other than highly committed parents and even they will be hard pressed to sustain their effort for long without intensive support.

Busy teachers must look for lightweight, low technology methods which are readily understandable, easily used in any brief available time and which require relatively simple and inexpensive materials or those already easily available. Given these features and succinct and straightforward training, high durability should be achieved, with a wide range of parents and peers proving able to successfully serve as tutors.

A crucial planning issue is where to draw the line between specificity and generality, between concreteness and abstraction. If your advice to tutors is very general and vague (in the hope that they can interpolate their helping 'across the curriculum' in all sorts of real-life situations), they may have grave difficulty operationalising it, i.e. they still won't know what it is you want them to do. On the other hand, if your training is very specific and rule-bound, the tutors may be effective but within a very narrow spectrum of operation, not producing effects which generalise.

The best compromise is to give some specific training initially, to ensure immediate success and confidence building for the tutors, then developing into more general training. For the same reasons, you may wish to supply or prescribe specific materials to support the tutoring at the outset, giving the participants increasing individual choice of materials later as a precursor to finding or making their own materials or being able to do without them. However, do not fall into the trap of becoming too preoccupied with materials – the important thing is for the interactions to be structured positively. Some materials may aid this but they will not guarantee it.

Whatever organisational format you adopt, the following considerations will be important. You will note that many of these are to do with structuring positive interaction.

Objectives

What benefits the programme is expected to have should be clearly articulated, not least for marketing/recruitment and subsequent evaluation purposes. The programme should not interfere with the school curriculum, but dovetail into it, while capitalising on the qualitative differences and advantages compared to regular teacher instruction. Keep the objectives modest for your first attempt.

Ability differential

Be clear with potential tutors (and yourself) about the degree of competence needed in the tutor and the feasible range of ability differential in the pair. Parents who are themselves hearing and/or language impaired may have great difficulty presenting children with a good model. In peer tutoring, for similar reasons you will probably opt for cross-ability tutoring, which may mean matching children of different ages from different classes or even different schools. While the tutor will usually be more able than the tutee, take care not to make the differential in ability too large or there will be little intellectual challenge involved for the tutor, who will then stand to benefit only socially and/or affectively from the process.

Flexibility
Procedures should preferably be applicable without major modification to participants of different ages and abilities with different life situations and needs and different learning styles. Clearly, heavy prescription of materials militates against these flexibility requirements. Likewise, the procedure should enable and facilitate the tutee to deploy a range of strategies, rather than strait-jacketing them into a single professionally preferred one. Activity should preferably be varied and multi-sensory, with alternation between different styles of reading, listening, writing, speaking, and so on.

Interaction
Procedures should involve responsive (inter-) activity from both members of the pair, since if one declines into being merely a checker or passive audience, motivation will soon evaporate. The procedure should promote a high rate of time on task, with an emphasis on keeping going – maintaining the flow of activity increases the number of learning opportunities and helps stave off anxiety.

Satisfaction
Likewise, both members of the pair must gain some intrinsic satisfaction from the activity, since pure altruism in the tutor will always expire eventually through boredom. Basically, it's got to be fun.

Self-management
The tutee should have a substantial degree of control over the process of tutoring and preferably over the curriculum content and materials as well. Tutee control of the amount of support offered by the tutor is especially valuable. Tutees should be able to exercise choice and initiative – deprived of the opportunity, they will never develop the skills.

Instructions
Should be simple, clear and above all *specific*. Instructions are probably best given as a series of finely task analysed steps. Parents (and peer tutors!) like to be told what they have to do to be right, at least at the start. Mostly they dislike wordy educational philosophising and vague and fuzzy open-ended statements. Both tutor and tutee should be given very clear (interactive) job descriptions, since without this the process of tutoring can rapidly degenerate into a muddle. The provision of a simple visual map, chart or other cue to remind the pair of how it is all supposed to work may well be helpful.

Materials

Especially for children with learning difficulties, the curriculum materials in use should be individualised to match the tutee's needs and interests, but are they to be completely free choice, controlled choice from ranges of difficulty or precisely specified by the professionals, or some continuum of these as the tutoring develops? Are the materials required actually available and easy for regular access by pairs? Does the tutoring procedure accommodate progression on to increasingly difficult materials? Do the materials themselves have extension activities inbuilt? Have you specified what the pair will need to have available by way of basic equipment (pen, paper, dictionary?) and ensured it will be available?

Error control

The tutee should not feel as if they are making many errors, since this is bad for morale. If this is not controlled via tutee-, tutor- or teacher-selected materials, careful accommodation by the tutor to the tutee's natural pacing and the provision of swift non-intrusive support must be a feature of the tutoring technique, without creating tutee dependency. Errors are potentially the major stress point in the tutoring relationship – but be alert to other possible causes of stress and fatigue in the system.

Error signalling

When an error is made, feedback should be swift that this is the case, but not so immediate that the tutee has no opportunity to detect the error themselves. Error signalling should be positive and minimally interruptive.

Error correction

A swift, simple, specific and preferably ubiquitously applicable error correction procedure must be clearly laid down, which is seen by the tutee as supportive and draws minimum attention to the error. There should be a strong emphasis on self-checking and self-correction, both higher order skills which need to be fostered.

Eliminate negatives

'Don't say don't' – rather than giving tutors a list of prohibited behaviours, prescribe positive error signalling and correction procedures which are incompatible with the undesirable negative and intrusive behaviours we all sometimes perpetrate.

Accentuate positives

Be specific about requirements for praise, including what to praise (especially self-correction and initiative-taking), frequency, verbal and non-verbal aspects, and the need for variety and relevance to the task. Deploy individual token or tangible rewards only if all else fails. Some group acknowledgement of participation via badges, certificates, etc. might be valuable and acceptable, and is useful advertising.

Discussion
Emphasise that discussion by the pair is essential to promote and confirm full understanding by the tutee, and is genuine work, to avoid mechanical conformity to the surface requirements of the task by either member of the pair.

Modelling
Ensure the tutoring procedure includes a demonstration of competence by the tutor which may be imitated (or improved upon) by the tutee, rather than over-reliance on verbal promptings. Tutors should also be encouraged to model more general desirable behaviours, such as enthusiasm for the topic in hand. Participant pairs will also serve as models for other pairs, and the project group should deliberately be kept in contact so that the social dynamic adds a further dimension to motivation. Remember the co-ordinating professional must model continuing enthusiasm for the programme!

Training
Training is essential, and should be done in vivo with both members of the pair present via verbal, visual and written information-giving (bilingual/signed if necessary) coupled with a demonstration, immediate practice, feedback, further coaching and subsequent monitoring. Training individual pairs separately is very costly, and well organised group training is as effective while also serving to develop group support and solidarity. You may need specially pre-selected materials or equipment for the training meeting.

Contracting
Specify an initial trial period and be very clear about the time costs for the pair should they participate. Remember little and often will be most effective, especially with tutees with learning difficulties. Expect pairs to clearly contract in to participation, which is of course voluntary but needs to be seen as total and not optionally partial. Ensure there is mutual feedback about effectiveness and proposed improvements by the end of the trial period. Discuss continuation options and seek contract renewal, possibly in a range of formats, by participants. At this point pairs should be increasingly confident and capable of devising their own adaptations and creating their own novelty, and should be increasingly ambitious.

Monitoring

Emphasise self-checking. Some simple form of self-recording is desirable, and both members of the pair should participate in this. Periodic checking of these records by the co-ordinating professional is a minimal form of accountability of high cost-effectiveness. This may need to be supplemented in at least some cases by verbal enquiry of one or both members of the pair and/or direct observation of the pair (and preferably other supplementary tutors) in action, either in school or at their home, in the first case either on an individual basis or in a group setting.

Evaluation

Be clear as to the objectives of evaluation, since there is little point in doing it for its own sake – what are you going to do with the results? Feeding back to the participants data on their success might increase their motivation. Publicising the data might expand subsequent recruitment or attract additional funding. How should you review to what extent the curriculum content of the tutoring has actually been mastered and retained in the longer term? Criterion-referenced tests closely allied to the tutoring process are likely to give the most valid (and most impressive) results, but a norm-referenced test in the same general area is a more stringent test of generalisation of skills acquired through tutoring and might be construed as more 'objective' by outsiders. You might also solicit subjective feedback from the participants on a consumer satisfaction basis, but design any questionnaire carefully to ask very specific questions and avoid inbuilt positive bias, since in any case you will benefit from the 'grateful testimonials' effect. Also remember to make it easy to score and summarise! Comparison or control groups are great if you can get them. Do try and save a little spare energy to collect longer term follow-up data on at least a sub-sample, to check on wash-out of gains. However, also ensure the evaluation procedure does not overwhelm or stress the participants – or indeed yourself!

Generalisation and maintenance

You will need to build in means for continuing review, feedback and injection of further novelty and enthusiasm if pairs are to keep going and maintain the use of their skills. Again, the social dynamic of the group is important. You are likely also to need to consciously foster their broadening the use of these skills to different materials and contexts for new purposes – all of this will consolidate the progress made, build confidence and empower the pair still further. When pairs have developed sufficient awareness of effective tutoring to begin to design their own systems, you know you have done a good job. As tutees themselves recruit a wider range of tutors, the tutee becomes even more central as quality controller of the tutoring process.

Further details of how to organise parent and peer tutoring projects (including planning proformas) will be found in Topping (1986 and 1988 respectively). Having warned of the dangers of overdependence on materials, let us now review some of those available.

Materials

Oracy is everywhere. Certainly parental involvement and peer tutoring projects nominally targeted on other curricular areas can involve a great deal of oracy work, as when parents and children discuss the solution of mathematical puzzles and games together, or children in class are involved in games for social and life skills as part of the personal and social education curriculum. Correspondingly, the range of materials which could be used to stimulate and promote oracy is potentially vast.

A great number of commercial publishers produce picture books (with minimal or no text) or series of picture cards (sequenced or not) which are intended for use in stimulating talk with young children. For slightly older children inset boards and jigsaws can provide endless opportunities for discussion, providing parents do not focus on task completion but instead on the value of the process (an excellent example here is the Talkabout fifty-piece giant floor jigsaws produced by Orchard Toys, which are extremely lively, detailed and humorous).

Many reading schemes now have supplementary activities and materials focusing on language development (e.g. Ginn 360) as a preparation for reading, although in relatively few cases are these materials designed also to be used by parents. More specifically, a number of language kits and programmes will be found in the catalogues of commercial publishers, and Taskmaster have produced a separate speech and language materials catalogue. Relatively little attention has been given to any possibility of usage by non-professional tutors, however.

Given the impossibility of dividing language from thought, a number of the 'thinking skills' programmes on the market can have strong implications for language development, and fortunately many include activities often used in co-operative peer pairs or small groups, although rarely with parents. Examples from Science Research Associates include the Thinklabs (Thinklab, Junior Thinklab, Thinklab 2) and the CoRT Thinking Programme.

Given the wealth of potential materials, it is an invidious task to make recommendations. Listed below are sources and resources particularly appropriate for parental involvement and peer tutoring applications, which are relatively easily and immediately usable. Materials should be selected to be enjoyable, to allow equally active co-operation (or competition!) between the pair, to be easy to understand, to encourage extended but task-focused discussion, to be flexible and allow extension activities, to be attractive and well packaged and to be inexpensive and preferably not look too much like 'schoolwork'. Three-dimensional materials are particularly appreciated by children of all ages. Also consider: durability, safety, brevity, manipulability, compactness and cohesion of components, size, quality of instructions, goal orientation, age appropriateness and multisensory aspects.

Materials for teachers

There are many general books for teachers in this area. For example, the Schools Council Communication Skills Project for children aged 7-13 years spawned a number of books and videos, e.g. Tough (1979). Downes (1978) produced a useful handbook for teachers of early years children. A very general guide was edited more recently by Wray (1990). The three 'Ways and Means' books published by Somerset LEA and Globe Education are a valuable resource for teachers working with language delayed children. However, here we shall concentrate on materials which include games and activities adaptable for parent and peer tutoring.

The Spoken Word Project Books 1-3 and *Teacher's Handbook*
R. Brown (1989) Edinburgh, Oliver and Boyd

Cambridge Primary Language Courses: talking and listening Levels 1-4
Althea (1986) Cambridge, Cambridge University Press
66 workcards plus teacher's notes

Learning through Talk: ideas from Bury classrooms
Bury Oracy Project (1989) Metropolitan Borough of Bury Education Department, Mark Street, Bury, Lancashire BL9 0BN

Talk It Over
S. Lane and M. Kemp (1987) London, Ward Lock
Books 1-4

Listen, Think and Speak
B. Norris, R. Hennessy and D. Harmer (1984) London, Cassell for Schools Council
Blue, green, red and yellow sections, teacher's book and activity master sheets

Teaching Talking: Teaching Resources Handbook
A. Locke and M. Beech (1991) Windsor: NFER Nelson

Brill the Brave: Primary Thinking Project 5-11
Questions Publishing
Based on Lipman's 'Philosophy for Children'

Developing Oral Skills
G. Brooks, J. Latham, and A. Rex (1986) London, Heinemann Educational
Photocopiable resource material and cassette, designed for small group work

Play Games with English
C. Granger. London, Heinemann Educational
Students' and teachers' books containing a graded collection of language games

Word Games with English
D. Howard-Williams and C. Herd (1986) London, Heinemann Educational

Language Express
Leeds, Arnold-Wheaton
Laminated cards and books with some interesting word games

Resources for Early Language Development
Centre for the Teaching of Reading (1982) University of Reading
Lists many pictorial resources

Look, No Words!
D. Manley. London, Longman for the SCDC
A guide to text-free materials which can be used to teach any language

Games for Language Learning (2nd edition)
A. Wright, D. Betteridge and M. Buckley (1984) Cambridge, Cambridge University Press
Don't be misled by the title – the general format is teacher presentation followed by pair or individual work

Handbook for Teachers: Language Development Activities
T. Bryans and S. Wolfendale (1979) Stafford, NARE

Activities and Games for Language Work
M. Leclerc (1983) Stafford, NARE

Listening and Speaking
W. Bindley and R. Griffiths (1976) Stafford, NARE

Games and Simulations in Action
A. Davison and P. Gordon (1978) London, Woburn Press

Also see commercial catalogues for many other possibilities.

Materials for parents

These are resources especially produced for parents.

Listen To Your Child
D. Crystal (1986) Penguin

Talking Together
STASS Publications, 44 North Road, Ponteland, Northumberland NE20 9UR
Loose-leaf folder of games and activities to promote attention, listening, speech and language. Sections on auditory attention, discrimination and memory, instruction following, story telling, etc. Suitable for lower primary

Supertalkers: Helping Your Child Learn to Talk
S. Colmar and K. Wheldall (1987) Positive Products, Cheltenham, Gloucestershire

Word Play: Language Activities for Young Children and Their Parents
S. Wolfendale and T. Bryans (1986) Stafford National Association for Remedial Education

Games and activities to develop language (Appendix 7) in *Teach Your Child to Read*
P. Young and C. Tyre (1985) London, Fontana

Games to Play to Help Your Child's Language
D. M. Jeffree. Hester Adrian Research Centre, University of Manchester

The First Words Language Programme
B. Gillham (1979) London, Allen and Unwin

Two Words Together
B. Gillham (1982) London, Allen and Unwin

Let Me Speak
D. Jeffree and R. McConkey (1976) London, Souvenir Press

Let's Talk: Learning Language in Everyday Settings
R. McConkey and P. Price (1986) London, Souvenir Press

Baby Talk
Rotherham Psychological Service
A video about parents' role in language development with children aged 0-2 years.

Talk Your Way to Reading: Helping your Child with Language
B. Cutting (1988) Leeds, Arnold

Talking Together: a practical guide for parents
L. Currie and C. Munro, Educational Psychology Service, Strathclyde
Parent booklet, video and training handbook for professionals. Targeted on preschool children. Activities categorised under: Opportunities for Talking, Asking Questions, Nursery Rhymes, Books, Pictures, Listening, Play and Memory Games

101 Good Picture Books
D. Reid (1988) Reading and Language Information Centre, University of Reading

Language and Learning: how can I help my child?
Language and Learning: how can I use finger play?
(1981) Reading and Language Development Centre, Nene College, Northampton

Materials for peers

Materials for peer tutoring and co-operative learning.

Everyman's Word Games
G. Brandreth (1986) London, Dent
160 paper and pencil word games, many highly suitable for upper primary and early high school pupils

Brain Puzzles
J. Tyler and G. Round. London, Usborne
Answers in the back! Ideal for co-operative problem solving pair work – bound to promote discussion. Suitable for upper primary and early high

Concept 7-9
Was available via Arnolds.
3 units including a variety of games and materials for pair work. For primary schools

A First Book of Board Games
D. Byrne. Modern English Publications
Dice and counters to supply. For 7-12 year olds

Games for Pairwork
J. Alstrop and D. Byrne. Modern English Publications
Dice and counters to supply. For 7-12 year olds

It's Your Turn
D. Byrne. Modern English Publications
Dice and counters to supply. For 7-12 year olds

Commercial games

Published interactive games involving spoken and written languages, useable for parental involvement and peer tutoring.

Play on WordZ, MB (Travel) 8+ yrs. Very simple word making from random combinations of 9 letters. Similar games include: Parker *Boggle,* 8+ yrs,16 letters, more elaborate and expensive; Crown Andrews *Just a Minute*, timing more elaborate; *Scrabble Dice*

Junior Dingbats, Waddingtons, 9+ yrs. Exploration of words and phrases graphically, figuratively, etc. Great fun but requires imagination

Junior Scrabble, 5-10 yr olds. Needs no introduction!

Word Rummikub, 8+ yrs. Letters on tiles. Form words from letters on your rack. You can dissemble words already on the table to make new words

Guess My Name, Ravensburger, 6-10 yrs. On a pictorial matrix, players give each other clues to the identity of a particular object/picture. Distributed in the UK by Fisher-Price

What's in the Square? Arnold. An attribute matrix yielding a classification, describing and guessing game.

Other commercial games suitable for high school children are available.

Ways forward

In this chapter we have considered the need for the development of parent involvement and peer tutoring in oracy in the current educational context, reviewed some of the research evidence indicating that it can work, outlined essential organisational issues and listed some relevant materials. Hopefully the action implications are clear, but sources of further more specific advice have been given in any case. All that is needed now is inspiration, motivation, concentration and application.

There is certainly a need for better quality, pragmatic action research in this area. Readers who successfully undertake projects along these lines and manage to build in some evaluation are invited to contact the author with a view to future collaboration and dissemination.

References

Bailey, J. S. et al. (1971) Modification of articulation errors of pre-delinquents by their peers. *Journal of Applied Behavior Analysis,* **4**, 265-81

Carpenter, R.L. and Augustine, L.E. (1973) A pilot training programme for parent-clinicians. *Journal of Speech and Hearing Disorders,* **38**, 48-58

Downes, G. (1978) *Language Development and the Disadvantaged Child.* London, Holmes McDougall for the Schools Council

Howlin, P. (1984) Parents as therapists: a critical review. In *Remediating Children's Language: Behavioural and Naturalistic Approaches,* ed. D. J. Muller. London, Croom Helm; San Diego, College-Hill Press

McDade, H. L. and Varnedoe, D. R. (1987) Training parents to be language facilitators. *Topics in Language Disorders,* **7(3),** 19-30

Miller, S. J. and Sloane, H. N. (1976) The generalization effects of parent training across stimulus settings. *Behavior Analysis,* **9(3),** 355-70

Mulac, A. and Tomlinson, C.N. (1977) Generalisation of an operant remediation programme for syntax with language delayed children. *Journal of Communication Disorders,* **10(3),** 231-43

Stevenson, P. et al. (1982) The evaluation of home based speech therapy for language delayed children in an inner city area. *British Journal of Disorders of Communication,* **17(3),** 141-8

Swinson, J. and Ellis, C. (1988) Telling stories to encourage language. *British Journal of Special Education,* **15(4),** 169-171

Topping, K. J. (1986) *Parents as Educators: Training Parents to Teach their Children.* London, Croom Helm

Topping, K. J. (1988) *The Peer Tutoring Handbook: Promoting Co-operative Learning.* London, Croom Helm

Tough, J. (1979) *Talk for Teaching and Learning.* London, Ward Lock and Drake

Weistuch, L. and Brown, B. B. (1987) Motherese as therapy: a programme and its dissemination. *Child Language Teaching and Therapy,* **3(1),** 57-71

Whitehurst, G.J. et al. (1972) Delayed speech studied in the home. *Developmental Psychology,* **7(2),** 169-77

Wray, D. (ed.) (1990) *Talking and Listening: Scholastic Handbook.* Leamington Spa, Scholastic

Classroom Conversations and Reflection

Judith Watson

Introduction

This chapter complements that which follows by Judith Scott. She considers classroom ethos and its effect on communication, using illustrative examples from our current research on reflective thinking and moderate learning difficulties. This chapter also provides excerpts of dialogue from the same extensive body of audio recordings, but here the focus is on the nature of teachers' talk with pupils, and on some of the activities teachers used to help their pupils develop their language and their thinking.

Several contributors to this book have emphasised the close relationship between thinking and language. Keith Topping notes that language is a form of thought and recommends the use of 'thinking skills' resources among others. Anne Macdonald stresses the contribution of problem solving and the fostering of hypothetico-deductive thinking towards pupils' independence in learning. Alison MacDonald and Caroline Rendle emphasise the increasingly rich symbolic levels being reached during imaginative doll play with their preschoolers. Morag Donaldson and Jennifer Reid refer to some activities which may enhance pupils' awareness of important functional aspects of communication like the roles of speakers and listeners, and reflection on the formal properties of language. They note that the contexts in which children need to deploy linguistic skills are 'not restricted to low level informal contexts'. Schools make demands on pupils to use 'disembedded' language from an early age. This is echoed by Ted Jefferies and Sally Dolan when they comment that talking should not be regarded as a skill to be developed without reference to what is being talked about. In school talking skills include explanation, exposition, audience awareness and (at least sometimes!) the communication of information that is genuinely new. And as Margaret Mason points out the SOED Listening and Talking attainments include the conveying of information, instructions and directions.

The following discussion is on ways in which teachers try to foster thinking during classroom dialogues involving pupils who have moderate learning difficulties. Difficulties in language use are widespread with such pupils. Restricted, relatively unsophisticated vocabularies, relatively immature sentence structure, and poor articulation are often accompanied by a marked lack of confidence in communication, and a tendency towards passivity and withdrawal in unfamiliar, taxing situations. Teachers are very aware of the emotional aspects of their pupils' difficulties in communication and of the importance of maintaining and enhancing their self esteem.

The aspects of teacher talk and classroom activities described here are relevant and potentially helpful to all pupils who experience difficulties in communication, for whatever reason.

Classroom talk by teachers

The conversations referred to in this paper form part of a large body of recordings reported on more fully elsewhere and in a report available from the present author.

One early aim of the research was to identify teacher talk with pupils that aimed to encourage them to be reflective. Examples are teachers asking pupils to justify their contributions, or teachers modelling their own thinking.

The classroom recordings were made during one school term in four special schools for pupils with moderate learning difficulties. In each school a teacher of pupils aged between ten and twelve years kindly agreed to participate. All were experienced teachers within special education. They were told by the researchers that the focus was on children's thinking during their usual planned curricular activities.

During each recorded classroom session, bounded by a break or a change in teacher, the teacher and one of two target pupils per class wore a radio microphone. The research assistant was an unobtrusive presence throughout, making contextual notes, and briefly discussing with the teacher her plans for the lesson beforehand, and her views on how it had gone, afterwards. The target pupils were also seen briefly after each session and asked what they had liked doing and whether they had found anything difficult and why.

From a sample of transcribed sessions from each classroom, teacher talk concerned with pupils' current class activity was extracted by the researchers for analysis. Straightforward management activities, and talking to other staff were excluded. All talk categorised was accessible to the target pupil in question: that is, it was audible, and directly addressed either to that pupil or to a group of which the pupil was part.

There were thus obtained over one thousand utterances, from sessions totalling approximately six hours per teacher. From these, categories of teacher talk were derived, by a process of repeated revision and refinement and crosschecking between the two researchers.

Six major categories emerged of which three were much the most prominent, representing 90% of the total. A consistent preferred style in all of the teachers' use of the three major categories was shown by the proportions in which these were employed across different sessions and by the stability of the rank ordering of their category usage.

The three major categories are outlined below, in order of frequency of usage.

Category 1
Teacher assesses pupil's knowledge and understanding of the current task. Usually this was by a straightforward question, e.g. 'Does anyone recognise that creature?'

Category 2
Teacher asks pupils to clarify, justify or explain their thinking: asks hypothetical questions, explores logical errors and contradictions and suggests strategies, e.g. 'If you were really the person who had to send out the fire engine what would you be checking up on?'

Category 3
Teacher provides general feedback and generally motivating comments concerning class activity but these are not specifically focused and contingent on pupil performance, e.g. 'I know it's a bit difficult for you but keep trying.'

All four teachers used the three main categories during teaching sessions, but to markedly different degrees. Two made very little use of the second category, which attempts to promote reflection by homing in on and often challenging what pupils say. This represented only 6% and 20% of their total talk, in comparison with over 40% in that of the other two teachers for whom this was the most frequently used category, and who had a correspondingly much lower proportion of the Category 1 utterances that dominated the talk of the former two teachers. Category 3 was more evenly distributed and represented 16% of total teacher talk. The remaining three types of teacher talk were infrequent.

Category 4
Teacher acts as model, thinking aloud, using strategies or making personal contributions, e.g. 'It's all terribly complicated for me to take in.'

Category 5
Teacher encourages independence and individuality in pupils, e.g. 'There's no right or wrong answers. It's what you think.'

Category 6
Teacher talk encourages peer contributions, judgements and assistance, e.g. 'She knows how to do it. She'll tell you.'

Clearly the finding that teachers in the study schools were using consistent styles is of great interest. The fact that they appeared across different curricular areas and with both of a teacher's target pupils indicates that they are characteristic of the teachers rather than dependent on a particular pupil or activity.

Did the preponderance within classrooms of certain kinds of teacher talk have a discernible effect on pupils? Were they themselves more likely to display reflection, in, for example the language they used, the way in which they reacted to new problem situations, or in focused dialogue in a contingent teaching situation?

This paper looks at evidence relevant to the above questions. First evidence of reflection in pupil talk is discussed. Then the length of classroom dialogues is related to teacher category use. Finally pupil responsiveness to a new classroom situation is related to their experiences in the classroom.

Pupils' reflective talk

From a small sample of session transcripts, talk by target pupils, whether when alone, with peers, or with the teacher, was identified as indicating reflection according to the following criteria.

1. Talk which included logical, causal or relational expressions, showing that pupils were linking ideas and considering the relationship between them. Examples occurred in all the four sessions examined. In peer conversations the focus was usually on progress on a task, as in 'I'm on a higher book than S'. Most comments of this kind, however, occurred in the context of class discussion, for example when a pupil was asked to clarify a news contribution.

2. Pupils expressed uncertainty, or made qualifying or hypothetical statements. All identified pupil talk of this kind occurred during whole class activity and none during individual work with a teacher. The session in which these pupil statements were most frequent was one in which they were engaged in role play.

3. Talk which referred to errors, difficulty, thought processes and strategies. Pupil talk in this category occurred most frequently when pupils were working as individuals and much consisted of comments to peers about the level of difficulty of their work. There were no instances of pupils asking each other for help, or talking more specifically about it to a peer.

During individual work in the sessions sampled there were no recorded examples of sustained dialogue between pupils that seemed to be extending or challenging their thinking. However, in this situation several teacher-pupil exchanges revealed tension. One target pupil went dashing ahead with work he could not understand and refused help from the teacher, another became dependent on the teacher, appearing to lose the confidence he had just shown in talking to his peers.

The recordings indicate that group activities were more facilitative of pupils' talking and thinking than the individual work which took up most of their time.

Dialogue in the classroom

One tape recorded classroom session was selected for each of the eight target pupils. In each case, as in the large majority of post session interviews, the teacher had said that the preceding session had been, in her view, satisfactory.

Dialogue sequences were identified from each of the session transcripts. These always included the teacher and the target pupil, and sometimes other pupils, and they focused on a particular topic. Such sequences were made up of conversational turns, utterances bounded either by a pause or by another person's utterance. Their identification was not unduly problematic from the typed transcripts, and the original tape recordings could be referred to where clarification was needed.

For each classroom dialogue sequence identified the number of turns was counted, note being made of the participants. Only sequences of three or more turns were included.

Fig. 12.1: Mean number of turns per sequence

Classroom 1		2		3		4	
8.1	11.6	7.25	7.4	7.0	7.0	16.0	30.1

Figure 12.1 indicates that both target pupils in Classrooms 1 and 4 experienced much longer dialogues on average with their teachers than those in Classrooms 2 and 3, although extended dialogue sequences did occur in all the classrooms. What is immediately noteworthy from the data is that the commonly observed three-turn IRF sequence (teacher initiates, pupil responds, teacher provides feedback) did not dominate these sessions. In Classroom 4 for example there were no such sequences. In this they differ from those so often reported as characteristic of many classrooms in primary schools where pupils are not showing such obvious

learning difficulties. Clearly the teachers were aiming to enhance and clarify their pupils' thinking and were using dialogue as one way of doing this. Several of the sequences were initiated by pupils.

Despite this encouraging finding many of the sequences were short and not apparently extending or challenging to the pupils. On examination it can be seen that the longer dialogue sequences occurred most prominently in the classrooms of those teachers who use a high proportion of Category 2 talk with their pupils. This was further investigated.

The convenient cut off point of nine turns was used to differentiate shorter from longer classroom dialogues. As Figure 12.2 indicates the percentage of Category 2 teacher talk was found to be 49% for longer and only 14% for shorter dialogue sequences when these were aggregated over all eight sessions. The indication is therefore, that teachers' frequent use of more probing demanding talk in their classroom results in longer dialogues with pupils that are focused on a topic.

Fig. 12.2: Categorised teacher talk in shorter and longer dialogue sequences (expressed as %)

	Cat 1	Cat 2	Cat 3	Cat 4	Cat 5	Cat 6
Longer sequences (9 turns or more)	39	49	9	0	1	2
Shorter sequences (less than 9 turns)	51	14	30	1	2	2

In longer dialogues, pupils play a more prominent role relative to the teacher than is the case with shorter ones. In Classroom 4 for example, 61% of the turns were produced by pupils, in contrast with only 48% in Classroom 3. It seems that the use of Category 2 did not, as might have been feared, inhibit pupils, resulting in short unsatisfactory dialogues. However, to judge their potential value we have to look at some examples. An obvious question of interest is whether the quality of pupils' thinking is enhanced by frequent experience of the kind of teacher talk which aims to encourage them to reflect and explain. Is there evidence in the data that they are developing habits of reasoning and reflection?

Three episodes illustrate characteristic features of shorter and longer classroom dialogues. The longer sequences have a high proportion of Category 2 teacher talk, more pupil participation and longer pupil utterances. Shorter classroom dialogues often contain monosyllabic utterances by pupils and a high proportion of teacher questions in Category 1.

The following interchange arose from a class activity in which pairs of pupils took turns to role play using the telephone to ask for assistance. The emphasis is on enhancing referential communication, developing pupils' skills as speakers and listeners. The one holding the red phone when the music stops begins by making a request.

[T = teacher. P = pupil. TP = target pupil. RA = research assistant.]
TP: Hello is the airport there?
P: No, you've got the wrong number.
T: No. We've had that one. We've used that idea.
TP: Is the airport there?
P: The aeroplane's left.
T: Right. Put the phones down please. How do you know which plane she is going to be phoning about? Listen, now that's two times that you have said things that block her, that don't let her talk, do you understand? You are making it hard for her, so let's try and do it differently. Let's see if you can help her to keep talking.
P: What aeroplane are you getting?
TP: I am going to France
P: Okay. It will be leaving at ten o'clock in the morning.
T: That was very good.

A typical short interchange in another classroom occurred when the teacher was testing pupils' memory for a story.

T: What's that picture of?
P: Leaves.
T: You were right the first time. What's that a picture of?
TP: A pile of leaves.
T: Good.

This extract comes from a tightly organised lesson using discussion of reading material which is focused to the extent that there is little opportunity to 'go beyond the given'. The story does refer to the protagonists' feelings and motivation but the pupils did not seem to be engaged or to identify with the story events.

A third extract from an extended dialogue comes from the morning news session in one classroom, where the teacher humorously picks up on an inconsistency.

TP: I am going to get new ones for my birthday.
T: What size are you J?
TP: A five and a six.
T: How can you be a five and a six?
P: I'm a five.
T: How can you be a five and a six? It must be quite hard to have two sizes of feet. Do your feet go up and down, are they sometimes big and sometimes small? Why do you say a five and a six? Is that because you're not sure?
TP: A five.
T: When you go for new shoes what size do you think you are going to be?

Unplanned situations, not part of the usual curricular experience of pupils, can also give us a useful indication of their response to challenge: in the four classrooms there was a new situation at the outset of the research project with the potential of arousing pupils' interest and curiosity. This was the introduction of the audio recording apparatus: radio-microphones to be worn by the teacher and a target pupil, and the presence of the research assistant who made observational notes and checked that recording was proceeding satisfactorily.

Naturally this was a considerable disruption to the normal routine, and it entailed a brief explanation by the teacher and research assistant to the class and target pupil concerned. The initial recorded session for each target pupil was considered likely to be unrepresentative, and was not used for detailed analysis. However the initial audio-tapes provide interesting examples of spontaneous questions and comments, hypotheses, explanations and practical experimentation by pupils. The following episodes of classroom dialogues illustrate some of these.

Classroom 1

The class was involved in practical science for much of the term, and pupils were practised in predicting what would happen, in testing their ideas, and giving explanations. There was a relaxed but lively atmosphere, and the frequent bursts of laughter on the tape convey a flavour of the pupils' enjoyment. The target pupil said in a brief discussion with the research assistant after the session that he had liked talking into the microphone and hearing the voices over the tape.

P: TP's not to touch them, eh?
TP: Are you recording them now?
RA: Yes, it's working nicely.
TP: Are these on?
RA: Yes.

TP: (examining dials) There's another two. That's the one that I've got, eh?
RA: That's the one that's linked to you and that's the one that's linked to Mrs J. In fact do you know why it makes that buzz? That's because they're very close together.
TP: If you stand near that one it'll buzz will it? Is it all right Miss? Stand near that one. Miss'll have to stand near that one, eh? Cos if I stand near that one it'll buzz. Miss it's awful big that tape recorder.
RA: It is a big one.
TP: What are these?
RA: That's for the headphone.
TP: Does a light come on on this Miss?
RA: No there's not a light on that one. It's a different sort.
TP: Miss is there a light on your one?

Classroom 2

The target pupil and the rest of her class initially showed mild curiosity concerning why she was given the microphone. When the second target pupil wore it, two weeks later, they asked a number of questions.

TP: (makes noises into the mike, blows and sings)
TP: There's no holes in this. How can they hear?
T: You're speaking into the mike.
P: When you speak in it your voice goes down there into the box. Goes down there into the thingummy.
P: But that's broken.
RA: No, that's the aerial. It's like your radio.

Classroom 3

This was a brisk task-oriented classroom with a relatively short time allocation. It was noticeable that pupils rarely asked other than basic procedural questions during class. They showed no curiosity about the recording but the target pupil appeared slightly apprehensive.

TP: Miss is that on. Miss?
T: I don't know.

This was the extent of reference to the novel situation in the classroom which because of time constraints had not been explained more generally to the class, either by the teacher or by the research assistant.

Classroom 4

In this classroom many group activities including much role play occurred. Pupils showed considerable interest in the reason for the target pupil wearing the microphone and proffered their own hypotheses.

P: Why do you need that on you?
P: If she didna she wouldna hear us.
T: Is there something wrong with her ears?
P: Aye, she willna hear us through that.
P: Aye, if you talk she'll still hear.
T: She doesn't hear through that. She hears with her...?
P: Ears.
T: It's not for listening. It's for the machine to listen.
P: So she willna hear us.
P: When we've finished can we listen to some?
T: Well, we'll have to talk about that later. There's some people who haven't given any news this morning.

Discussion

The most obvious feature of the talk typically experienced by pupils in the different classrooms lay in the relative proportions of Categories 1 and 2. Category 1 consisted mainly of direct questioning and focused on current work and its successful completion, but teachers also linked pupils' knowledge to their other experiences in and out of school, outlined procedures and summarised progress. By these valuable means teachers aimed to clarify and enhance pupils' classroom activity but they did not challenge or extend them to 'go beyond the given'. As noted, Category 1 teacher talk was predominant throughout the classrooms where the average length of pupil-teacher dialogues was shorter and pupil contributions less prominent. This kind of teacher talk occurred in all four classrooms and particularly at the beginning of each session. In two of the classrooms as already noted, the more probing, demanding teacher talk represented in Category 2 then became prominent, as pupils were asked to predict, explain, justify. These teachers judged 85% and 100% of their respective sessions to have been challenging to their target pupils. They viewed such challenge positively: 'She disagreed with the others who were wrong,' and, 'Lovely enthusiasm for language at which he was hesitant initially.' This contrasted with the remark by another teacher, 'We stop before it gets too hard,' who judged that only 20% of the sessions had been challenging to the target pupil.

Pupils' own talk showed the beginning of metacognitive and metacommunicative awareness, in their expressions of doubt, comments on task difficulty and occasional strategic behaviour like checking and planning. This was likely to be enhanced by teachers explicitly pointing out sources of confusion as in, 'Check up because people don't hear things. They make mistakes so always double check,' or in modelling reflective thinking themselves, 'No, I didn't understand that bit. Shall we have another wee look at that one?'

In the transcripts generally there were rather infrequent examples of peers' opinions, evaluations and help being deliberately enlisted by teachers. It is notable however, that some of the times when pupils were most animated and involved were when they were engaged in joint activities with their classmates. Examples include practical science and model making, problem solving and role playing. These were the situations that elicited hypothetical, imaginative and logical language from pupils to a much greater extent than when pupils were engaged in individual activity. Individual work occupied most of pupil time but did not in practice appear to be a challenging context. Unplanned and novel experiences also naturally arouse pupils' curiosity. Pupils' first encounters with the recording apparatus resulted in spontaneous questioning and conjectures in those classrooms where problem solving, explaining and an encouragement to reflect were part of their everyday classroom experience, and prominent features of their teacher's talk.

Margaret Donaldson's work on the interrelationships and development of language and thinking has had an impact on educational practice and on the study of child development which extends way beyond her native Scotland. *Children's Minds*, published in 1978, shows how education emphasises pupils' ability to reflect on abstract ideas, their awareness of their own thought processes and language, and the ability to analyse and manipulate ideas.

This chapter has attempted to show some ways in which teachers engage in the delicate task of providing experiences of sufficient challenge to extend pupils' language and thinking without losing their interest or reducing their confidence.

Communicating Context: a tangled web

Judith Scott

Introduction

This paper has grown and evolved out of the study of a whole drawerful of tape recordings of normal classroom teaching sessions where the focus was on the teacher and pupil talk, and where the research was investigating the degree to which the pupils thought reflectively and the degree to which teachers encouraged reflective thinking in their pupils. After many hours listening and transcribing the tapes, it became more than apparent that the dialogue that was written on the page was less than half the story, the important bits that were missing were the unseen and unheard past, the bit that had gone before, and the 'feel' of the classroom. In other words the context from which the written dialogue had been extracted was such an important part of the story that it could not be ignored. It is this context that this paper is proposing to address in an attempt to put some flesh on the abstract notion of the classroom environment or culture . . . or ethos . . . or 'feel'.

This brings us to the first difficulty which is one of defining what exactly is meant by this abstract notion of ethos or culture. Each person tends to have their own idea of what they mean by this 'feel' or sense of the atmosphere, and any definition tends to narrow the concept. It is, however, the breadth of the concept that is both its strength and its weakness. Chambers Concise Dictionary defines ethos as, 'the distinctive habitual character and disposition of an individual, group, race, etc.' Culture, in the sense that we are using it, is defined as, 'the attitudes and values which inform a society'. It is somewhere between these two definitions that captures the closest essence of the context that is being addressed in this paper, where the distinctive character and disposition of the school, in the material sense, is integrated with the attitudes and values prevalent among the school community. Another dimension is added to the concept by Cusick (1985) who sees this 'something' as the schools' 'vision' of themselves, where there is:

> a vision contained within schools, a vision that the community and staff have of themselves, the students, the future state of the students, and the relations between these elements. That vision is reflected in and makes intelligible the teaching, the curriculum, and the activities schools undertake.

The subjective nature of the concept is raised further when attempting to define a 'good' or positive ethos or culture within a classroom. In general terms this has been taken to be an atmosphere that appears to promote the self esteem of all the pupils in the classroom, where they are encouraged to see themselves and each other in a positive light, where they feel that they themselves and their ideas are valued, where there is a non-judgemental acceptance of each pupil's worth, where there is a relaxed, but controlled, sense of purpose, calmness and security.

This paper looks at teacher talk and pupil talk from classrooms where there appeared to be this positive ethos, where there was a good 'feel' within the classroom, and discusses examples and incidents that would appear to promote, control and maintain the atmosphere within the classroom. This is in no way a comprehensive approach and is put forward as a basis for discussion, as observations on practice within the classroom where the ethos of the whole school and the classroom appear integrated, supportive, consistent, purposeful and positive.

In looking at episodes of teacher and pupil talk this chapter is taking a very narrow perspective on the climate of a classroom. The atmosphere in the classroom itself is influenced by the school environment in which it rests, there are physical and material aspects to a school and classroom climate, there are organisational aspects, there are wider social and economic influences; in short the atmosphere/ethos in a classroom is a product of a full range of micro and macro influences. Rutter, in his seminal work, suggests that the '*cumulative* effect of . . . various social factors was considerably greater than the effect of any of the individual factors on their own', and he continues, 'the implication is that the individual actions or measures may combine to create a particular *ethos*, or set of values, attitudes and behaviours which will become characteristic of the school a whole' (Rutter, 1979). Teacher and pupil talk is therefore only one particular aspect of this 'ethos, or set of values, attitudes and behaviours', but the examples investigated later in the chapter perhaps indicate at the same time the presence of wider influences and approaches within their school settings.

Is 'ethos' just another buzz word?

Within the educational field there is an increasing interest in the ethos of schools, involving a variety of disciplines and approaches. From the educational research approach, Rutter's work, referred to above, initiated the idea that the 'school effect' was a significant factor in pupil behaviour and attainments. This may seem a commonplace assumption now, but at the time when the study was started there was 'widespread acceptance among academics that schools made little difference' (Rutter, 1979). From here, research attention then focussed on the extent to which ordinary schools vary in their effects on children's cognitive performance (Rutter, 1985).

Within the child development and the psychological fields there has been a similar move towards acknowledging the importance of the context in which development was occurring. John Nisbet points out that, within research on teaching and learning to think, the most interesting trend has been the recognition that thinking is not purely cognitive, but involves affective factors – feelings, values, attitudes and motivation. Nisbet argues that intelligence is not innate or unchangeable, and suggests that 'powerful learning environments' may be created to improve intelligence and accelerate cognitive development (Nisbet, 1990).

From the educational research field Boekaerts argues strongly that it is 'high time that affective variables are considered more fully in educational research and that a systematic attempt is made to apply findings in the fields of motivation, anxiety, stress, coping and social support to educational practice' (Boekaerts, 1988). She suggests that the cognitive processing approach has resulted in drawing attention away from the real learner in the classroom 'with his (sic) motives and goals, his interest and liking, his stress and frustration; and above all his tendency to make compromises'. Boekaerts continues by discussing several different lines of research that show evidence of a relationship between emotion, motivation and learning. It is at this level of beginning to address these affective variables of feelings, values, attitudes and motivation that this paper is investigating a part of the context within which teaching and learning occur in the classroom.

In addition, the promotion of good management within education has led to the development of a set of performance indicators that include a number of indicators relating to school ethos. HMI, who developed these indicators, have commented on the 'good tone, atmosphere, spirit or ethos' in schools which are 'well led and where teaching and learning are effective and relationships are well handled' (SOED, 1992). The twelve ethos indicators identified refer to the whole school experience and although none of the indicators stands on its own, the focus in this paper is more on three of them: pupil morale, the learning context and teacher-pupil relationships. In an interesting slant, it is suggested that pupil morale is the most significant ingredient in the success of a school; it may equally be suggested that this is important for the pupils themselves. The focus is on the degree to which 'pupils enjoy school and feel that what they are learning is interesting and relevant'. Within the learning context, with the implication that this means the classroom, focus is on the expectations that both teachers and pupils bring to it, and on how they relate to one another within it. This overlaps with the indicator that addresses teacher-pupil relationships, where these are seen to cover 'a range of possibilities including the nature of the social relationship as well as the teacher-learner relationship, and encompasses mutual respect, tolerance, the approachability of teachers, the goodwill of pupils, and expectations that each bring to the situation' (SOED, 1992). Harmonious relations between teachers and pupils and the degree of courtesy and respect are suggested to be evidence of the 'ethos' prevailing in the learning context.

In their study of probationers, Draper et al. (1991) point to comments made on the importance of school ethos as a supportive factor. Although this is not investigated further in the report, it does indicate that school ethos affects the teacher, and particularly the probationer; this further widens the implications for investigating and debating the issue of school ethos.

If nothing else, this preamble may indicate the complex nature of the topic, and give some sense of what is being addressed. At the same time it is hoped that the positive qualities of the classrooms from which the following examples have been taken have also emerged. Much of what has been addressed cannot be explicitly illustrated by taking excerpts of 'talk', but the quality of the teacher-pupil relationships and the degree of respect and courtesy involved are arguably both explicitly and implicitly illustrated.

The fly on the classroom wall

The classrooms, from which the following taped sessions were selected, were in special schools catering for pupils with moderate learning difficulties. The classes consisted of ten or eleven pupils, boys and girls, aged between ten and eleven. Within this, each class had children with a variety of social, emotional, behavioural and physical difficulties.

The following excerpts of teacher and pupil talk are taken from classrooms where the ethos or culture appeared to be positive for pupils and teacher, and at the same time the whole school ethos or culture appeared to include many of the criteria discussed in the previous section. One of the striking aspects of these classrooms was the degree of respect that the teachers had for their pupils as individuals in their own right; this respect was shown in many ways, but from the point of view of gathering data and being able to provide an illustration this can only be shown by verbal communication taken from the transcripts. Respect in this sense involved the teacher encouraging the pupils to have consideration for each other, the teacher modelling how to be considerate by her own approach to her pupils. Respect in a wider sense was approached through discussion of gender and race issues and also in a discussion on death. Another noticeable factor within these classrooms was the consistency of approach of the teachers.

The first examples are all incidents selected from one morning session of normal classroom activities, and are placed in the order in which they occurred. The issues appear randomly and it is interesting to note that the teacher is prepared to take all the opportunities to address issues as they arise.

The first short excerpts occur while the teacher and the majority group in the classroom are having a discussion: the teacher asks the permission of the pupils to interrupt their discussion in order to control and manage the two other pupils in the classroom. (The pupils' names have been changed in all these examples.)

Discussion between teacher and group of pupils:

Teacher:	Can we just stop a wee minute while I sort Claire and Malcolm out.

Teacher moves across room to sort out problem, before returning to continue discussion with the group.
Discussion continues.
And again a few minutes later:

Teacher:	Claire, what are you doing. (Raised voice)
Teacher:	Excuse me. (Quietly, to group she has been talking to.)

Teacher then moves across room to deal with problem.

In asking the pupils' permission to interrupt the group work, the teacher indicates both respect for the pupils and that what they have been doing is important. As it is, the group sit quietly and wait while the disruption is being dealt with.

Later, during the course of the same morning, the issue of respect for others emerged involving the social aspects of race and gender, interspersed with the teacher encouraging pupils to respect each other within the classroom.

Pupils and teacher have been looking at four different pictures of people eating a meal and discussing what they saw. A pupil pointed out that the people in one picture had black hair . . .

Pupil:	They're Paki.
Teacher:	Could you use the word Pakistani that Karen used, 'cos it's nicer. Would you like us to call you a 'Scottie'?
Pupil	Nuh.
Teacher:	No, you're Scottish, that's the proper word. So let's use the word Pakistani or Indian. They might be Indian.

Discussion continues . . .
A few minutes later . . .

Teacher:	I'm sorry.
Teacher:	It really is very hard to hear what Rachel says, and it's specially hard if other people are talking at the same time.

Teacher: Rachel sat very quietly when you were talking Patrick . . .

Pause.
All silent.

Teacher: Thank you.

Discussion then continues . . .
A few minutes later . . .
Discussion about the pictures of people eating meals continues . . .

Teacher: OK, another question. Let's look at the green picture. I'd like everyone's ideas on this. Who cleans this kitchen?
Louise: The lady.
Teacher: Umm. (Pause) Hands up.
Teacher: Who cleans this kitchen, Patrick?
Patrick: The mum.
Teacher: The mum.
Teacher: What do you think, Kirsty?
Kirsty: The mum.
Teacher: Linda?
Linda: The dad. (Laughter)
Teacher: He cleans the kitchen.
Teacher: Why did you laugh?
Louise: Dads don't . . . some dads don't clean the kitchen. It's always the mum.
Teacher: Some dads don't clean the kitchen. It's always the mums?
Teacher: What do you think, Helen. Who do you think cleans this kitchen?
Helen: The mummy.
Teacher: Rachel, who cleans this kitchen?
Rachel: The mum and the dad.
Teacher: The mum and the dad.
Rachel: Yes.
Teacher: Do they do it together?
Rachel: No.
Teacher: Tina, who cleans this kitchen?
Tina: The lady in the house, the dusting and that . . .
Teacher: So what do you think about that? Louise laughed when Linda said the daddy cleans the kitchen. (Laughter)

Teacher: Your daddy and mummy both clean the kitchen?
Linda: Yeh.
Tina: Ma dad and me clean the kitchen. Ma mum and my sister clean the living room.
Teacher: Right, so your dad does help clean, right. So what do you think about that?
Louise: Fine.
Tina: No bad.
Teacher: So you think that's fine.

The discussion continues, and in a gentle way the issue has been seriously addressed and examined and all pupils have been included in the discussion.

On another occasion the following discussion took place. This arose during a game of 'musical telephones' which was to encourage the pupils both to communicate with each other and to communicate using the telephone. Two pupils were left holding telephones when the music stopped, the pupil with the red phone had to think of a person or organisation (auntie, friend, police, local 'take-away', etc.) to ring, and the pupil with the black phone had to pretend to be that person, and between them they had to construct the conversation.

Pupils and teacher playing game of 'musical telephones' . . .

Tina: Hello, is that the hospital please?
Louise: Yes, it is.
Tina: I've phoned to see if my wee girl is OK.
Louise: No, she's died.
Tina: Ah.

Silence.

Teacher: Louise would you make this like a real phone call, would you do that on the phone to somebody . . .
(Linda: You've said your daughter's died.)
Teacher: Just put the phone down a minute please while we talk about this. Would you do that to somebody? (Louise: No.) No, I hope you wouldn't and I hope nobody ever does it to you, what a terrible thing. That does happen to people sometimes that their children are getting very ill and sadly sometimes they do die. What do you think people in hospital do if they have a child who dies, how do you think they tell the mums and dads? They don't phone up and tell them.

Helen: They wait till the mum comes in and then they tell her.
Teacher: They would phone up and say please come to the hospital we need to talk to you. You would never, ever talk like that on the phone, Louise. Can we start that phone call again. Right, start from the beginning.
Tina: Hello, is that the hospital?
Louise: Yes, please come down, I'd like to talk to you and your husband please.
Tina: Is it important?
Louise: Yes it is.
Tina: OK, I am just coming.
Teacher: Good. (Music starts)

Again in a gentle, but firm, manner, respect for people's feelings was addressed and discussed; the issue was not ignored.

In another situation and classroom, respect is created and maintained in a more implicit rather than explicit manner. One way that demonstrates this is in how knowledge about home and family is put on an equal footing; it is not a one-way process of teacher expecting pupils to tell her about their family doings and news on demand, it is a give and take process which is genuine, voluntary and non-judgemental.

Class news time, where pupils and teacher are sitting around in a circle ...

Teacher: . . . Good, is there anything else that has been happening last night that you want to tell us about?
Teacher: Did I tell you that Scott got a mouse this weekend, remember I told you we got a cat and a little kitten? Do you think it is a good idea to have a mouse as well if you've got a cat?

Discussion, about what might happen if you have a cat and mouse in the same house, follows.

The teacher has given her news as part of the class news time. Her news is part of a longer-term dialogue, where she had obviously talked about the cat before, and there was also no need to explain that Scott was one of her own family, so that basic knowledge about family backgrounds was assumed to be shared by everyone.

With this background of having revealed a glimpse of her own family the teacher later on in the same session is able to ask about the people at the home of a pupil and to probe mildly, without any sense of threat or demand.

Talking about models they have made in the classroom . . .

Teacher:	Did they like your car when you took it home?
Teacher:	What did Alastair say?
Pupil:	He says, he went . . . (indistinct)
Teacher:	Did he? That's super.
Teacher:	And what about you Stuart? What did your mum and your ... what's his name, Andrew, is it Andrew?
Stuart:	Andy.
Teacher:	Andy. What did he say about the car? Did they like it?

In this case the teacher is also indicating awareness and acceptance to the pupil of their particular home circumstances.

Humour and fun were an important part of the communicating process in this classroom, and again the fact that it was part of a two-way process took away any sense of threat to the pupil. The following example was part of a long session in which, building on a story the pupil had read in his reading book, the pupil had to think up and draw items to put into a cauldron in order to make up a witch's spell, and then make up magic words to accompany the spell. The teacher encouraged and cajoled the pupil to do this on his own, but he did not find use of his imagination and free thinking easy; the time span shows the degree of his difficulty, in that he has been set his task approximately thirty-five minutes before the following interaction occurs.

Teacher:	I'm going to see Johnny for a minute. How are you doing?
Teacher:	Right, so what's your magic words?
Johnny:	Uh . . .

Pause.

Teacher:	Goodness me, all this stuff will have boiled away to nothing by the time you have said your magic words. Let's leave the magic words for a minute if you're not sure. Is it because you can't think of any? Well do you want to put down some words that you know?
Teacher:	What magic words do you know?
Johnny:	Abracadabra.

A few moments later, after Teacher has dealt with another pupil.

Teacher: Good. Abracadabra.
Teacher: What's your spell for?
Teacher: Now what are you going to do with this spell? Is there anything you would like to get rid of or change?

Pause.

Teacher: Apart from magic the teacher into a frog, is that what you would like to do?
Johnny: What?
Teacher: Magic your teacher into a frog.
Johnny: Aye.
Teacher: Would you? Oh, then where would you be without me I wonder?
Johnny: We would do all the work.
Teacher: You'd do all the work would you?
Johnny: I'd . . . finish all the books.
Teacher: So you would magic the teacher into a frog and you would do all the work with the magic spell would you? You would tidy up the room as well would you Johnny?
(Pupil: That's a good idea.)
Johnny: . . . and water the plants . . .
Johnny: . . . And change the classroom.
Teacher: What would you change the classroom into?

The conversation continues in this vein.

Here, gently teasing the pupil, by suggesting that everything 'will have boiled away to nothing by the time you have said your magic words', doesn't spur him on. However, when the tables are turned and the teacher puts herself at the receiving end of the humour, the pupil's imagination is fired and suggestions come pouring out.

The fun also emerges in the next excerpt, where the teacher and pupil laugh together over the pupil's efforts to read sentences from his workbook.

Teacher and pupil going over sentences in work book. . .

Johnny: I know what to do.
Teacher: What is that word?

Johnny:	I know.
Teacher:	What . . . does it say, the word . . .
Johnny:	Don't . . .
Teacher:	Rubbish. (Mock stern voice)
Johnny:	(Laughs)
Johnny:	Dragon.
Teacher:	Oh . . . Oh . . . no . . . (Laughs)
Teacher:	Let's read the sentence 'n see if that helps.
Johnny:	Right, I know.
Teacher:	Read the first sentence.
Johnny:	The book was about . . . about . . .
Teacher:	Ye - e - s . . . about, about . . .
Johnny:	. . . a . . . dragon. (Funny voice)
Teacher:	or . . .
Johnny:	The book was about a tr . . . (laughs) a tree.

Teacher and pupil laugh together.

Johnny:	Now, now. . .
Johnny:	This . . .

Pause.

Johnny:	(tries again) Pirates.
Teacher:	Come on, read the sentences.
Johnny:	I know.
Teacher:	You don't know.
Johnny:	I do

Pause.

Johnny:	There, that . . .
Teacher:	What is the right sentence then?

Conversation continues, then Johnny works on his own.
A few minutes later Teacher returns to look at pupil's work . . .

Teacher:	What does that say?
Johnny:	Tail . . . belt.
Teacher:	A what?

Johnny: . . .round a tree.
Teacher: . . . and a?
Johnny: . . . a dr . . . tail.
Teacher: . . . a belt round a tail, right?
{ Johnny: Aw naw . . . Tick them (laughing)
Teacher: This is . . .
Johnny: Tick them.
Teacher: What does that say?
Johnny: A trip . . . What have I done here?
Teacher: (Laughing)
Johnny: (Laughs) It isn't funny.
Teacher: (Laughing)
Johnny: I've done that . . . funny.
Teacher: What should it . . . what does it say?
Johnny: A dragon under a tree.
Teacher: Uh ha. (Conversation continues . . .)

Within the fun the pupil is able to see that he has made a mistake and to admit that he has 'done that . . . funny'.

These few examples may give a flavour of the type of exchanges that are taking place in classrooms where there is a positive ethos, where respect between teacher and pupil exists, and where the self-esteem of the pupil is encouraged. It is hoped that it can be seen that each of these exchanges cannot be taken in isolation, that they would not be effective if they were not part of the whole school approach, and also if they were not part of the historic process of the individual classroom. In other words, these examples are both the *result* of a positive ethos as well as the *means of creating* this indefinable 'ethos'.

Conclusion

As an aside from the research, after spending time in school classrooms, it became apparent that teachers often feel isolated in their classrooms and do not have the means of being a fly on the wall in other classrooms, nor is there much opportunity for discussions with fellow professionals. This is an attempt to show in a small way what happens in 'other' classrooms, and to open up the discussion on the ethos/culture/atmosphere within the classroom. In particular in relation to communication, where a sense of respect and a sense of equality clear the channels of what is a two-way process.

This paper should be seen as a set of observations that emerged from research into communication in the classroom, where the indefinable ethos or climate or context appeared to be a significant factor in the effectiveness of the classroom communication.

Throughout this paper various terms have been used, perhaps confusingly, to refer to the subject – context, ethos, culture, environment, learning environment, affective variables, vision, feel, atmosphere, school effect, climate. This is not to argue that all these words may be used interchangeably, but to suggest that, although they may be used within different disciplines and approaches, they all form part of the same whole which, perhaps because it is difficult to define and address, is not given the full attention it merits.

References

Boekaerts, M. (1988) Emotion, motivation and learning. *International Journal of Educational Research,* **12**

Cusick, P. (1985) Finding meaning in teaching. *Education and Urban Society,* **17**

Draper, J., Fraser, H., Smith, D., and Taylor, W. (1991) *A Study of Probationers.* Edinburgh, Moray House Institute of Education

Nisbet, J. (1990) Teaching thinking: an introduction to the research literature. *Spotlights,* **26**. Edinburgh, Scottish Council for Research in Education

Rutter, M. et al. (1979) *Fifteen Thousand Hours.* Cambridge, Massachusetts, Harvard University Press

Rutter, M. (1985) Family and school influences on cognitive development. *Journal of Child Psychology and Psychiatry and Allied Disciplines,* **26**

Scottish Office Education Department. (1992) *Using Ethos Indicators in Primary School Self-Evaluation.* Edinburgh, HMSO

Contributors

Dorothea Bogle is lecturer in Phonology, Language Studies Department, Moray House Institute of Education.

Lynda Booth is a senior special education teacher seconded to the MicroCentre at Dundee University.

Sally Dolan is a senior educational psychologist with Strathclyde Regional Psychological Service (Glasgow Division) based in Bridgeton Office.

Dr Morag L. Donaldson is a lecturer in the Department of Psychology, University of Edinburgh.

Dr Peter Gregor is a lecturer in Computer Science at the University of Dundee MicroCentre.

Dr Edward Jefferies is a senior educational psychologist with Strathclyde Regional Psychological Service (Glasgow Division) based in Central Office.

Alison MacDonald is employed part-time in the Department of Speech Pathology and Therapy, Queen Margaret College, Edinburgh and part-time as a specialist speech and language therapist at New Trinity Centre (Scottish Council for Spastics), Edinburgh.

Anne Macdonald is assistant headteacher (special educational needs) at Fintry Language Unit, Dundee.

Margaret McGregor is a specialist speech and language therapist in the Primary Language Unit, Cedarbank, West Lothian.

Gregor McMillan is an educational psychologist in Lothian Region, based in the Drylaw Office in Edinburgh.

Margaret Mason is senior language support teacher for the Borders Region, based in Philiphaugh Primary Schook, Selkirk.

Dr Anne O'Hare is a consultant pediatrician in Community Child Health, and honorary consultant for paediatric neurology at the Royal Hospital for Sick Children, Edinburgh. She has a special interest in educational neurology.

Jennifer Reid is a speech and language therapist who is currently working as a research fellow in the Department of Psychology, University of Edinburgh.

Caroline Rendle is employed by the Edinburgh Child Health Unit as a specialist speech and language therapist at Graysmill School.

Judith Scott is currently a research assistant working with Judith Watson on reflective thinking and moderate learning difficulties.

Dr Keith Topping is Director of the Centre for Paired Learning and of the MSc in Educational Psychology in the Department of Psychology, University of Dundee.

Mo Townson was class teacher in a primary language unit, and is now depute headteacher, Mayfield Primary School, Dalkeith.

Dr Judith Watson lectures and researches on special educational needs at Moray House Institute of Education.

Meeting Special Educational Needs: A Scottish Perspective

Series Editors: Gwynedd Lloyd and Judith Watson

Volume 1: ***Innovatory Practice & Severe Learning Difficulties***
Edited by Judith Watson

Ideas and information for professionals, parents and staff who are concerned with pupils with severe learning difficulties in special and mainstream settings.

1991 184pp ISBN 0 90158 036 8 £10

British Journal of Special Education:
This collection represents research and practice which are excitingly new... well worth the purchase price.

Volume 2: ***Chosen with Care? Responses to disturbing and disruptive behaviour***
Edited by Gwynedd Lloyd

Examines professional approaches to children and young people whose behaviour has been seen as disruptive or disturbing in school.

Describes current practice in a range of settings from 'secure' provision through residential and day special units to systems of support for pupils in ordinary school.

1992 153pp ISBN 0 90158 047 3 £10

Times Educational Supplement:
Invaluable in its practical and authoritative information and reasoned analysis... it will provide solid support for all those who are committed to choosing to care.

Volume 3: ***Special Educational Needs Beyond 16***
Edited by Alison Closs

Examines the background to the rapid increase in numbers of young people and adults with special educational needs in continuing education.

Describes developments – many of them innovative – in schools, FE colleges and other establishments and agencies.

1993 203pp ISBN 0 90158 059 7 £12.50

Volume 4: ***A Curriculum for All? 5-14 and Special Needs***
Edited by Elizabeth Jordan

Addresses the concerns of practitioners at all levels who are currently reviewing practice to ensure that the 5-14 Guidelines are used appropriately in planning teaching and learning in Scottish schools.

Examines philosophy, policy and practice in the provision of a curriculum to include all pupils.

Of interest to all in education.

April 1994 ISBN 0 90158 062 7 £12.50